C-377   CAREER EXAMINATION SERIES

This is your
PASSBOOK for...

Investigator

Test Preparation Study Guide
Questions & Answers

COPYRIGHT NOTICE

This book is SOLELY intended for, is sold ONLY to, and its use is RESTRICTED to individual, bona fide applicants or candidates who qualify by virtue of having seriously filed applications for appropriate license, certificate, professional and/or promotional advancement, higher school matriculation, scholarship, or other legitimate requirements of education and/or governmental authorities.

This book is NOT intended for use, class instruction, tutoring, training, duplication, copying, reprinting, excerption, or adaptation, etc., by:

1) Other publishers
2) Proprietors and/or Instructors of "Coaching" and/or Preparatory Courses
3) Personnel and/or Training Divisions of commercial, industrial, and governmental organizations
4) Schools, colleges, or universities and/or their departments and staffs, including teachers and other personnel
5) Testing Agencies or Bureaus
6) Study groups which seek by the purchase of a single volume to copy and/or duplicate and/or adapt this material for use by the group as a whole without having purchased individual volumes for each of the members of the group
7) Et al.

Such persons would be in violation of appropriate Federal and State statutes.

PROVISION OF LICENSING AGREEMENTS – Recognized educational, commercial, industrial, and governmental institutions and organizations, and others legitimately engaged in educational pursuits, including training, testing, and measurement activities, may address request for a licensing agreement to the copyright owners, who will determine whether, and under what conditions, including fees and charges, the materials in this book may be used them. In other words, a licensing facility exists for the legitimate use of the material in this book on other than an individual basis. However, it is asseverated and affirmed here that the material in this book CANNOT be used without the receipt of the express permission of such a licensing agreement from the Publishers. Inquiries re licensing should be addressed to the company, attention rights and permissions department.

All rights reserved, including the right of reproduction in whole or in part, in any form or by any means, electronic or mechanical, including photocopying, recording, or by any information storage and retrieval system, without permission in writing from the Publisher.

Copyright © 2024 by
National Learning Corporation

212 Michael Drive, Syosset, NY 11791
(516) 921-8888 • www.passbooks.com
E-mail: info@passbooks.com

PUBLISHED IN THE UNITED STATES OF AMERICA

PASSBOOK® SERIES

THE *PASSBOOK® SERIES* has been created to prepare applicants and candidates for the ultimate academic battlefield – the examination room.

At some time in our lives, each and every one of us may be required to take an examination – for validation, matriculation, admission, qualification, registration, certification, or licensure.

Based on the assumption that every applicant or candidate has met the basic formal educational standards, has taken the required number of courses, and read the necessary texts, the *PASSBOOK® SERIES* furnishes the one special preparation which may assure passing with confidence, instead of failing with insecurity. Examination questions – together with answers – are furnished as the basic vehicle for study so that the mysteries of the examination and its compounding difficulties may be eliminated or diminished by a sure method.

This book is meant to help you pass your examination provided that you qualify and are serious in your objective.

The entire field is reviewed through the huge store of content information which is succinctly presented through a provocative and challenging approach – the question-and-answer method.

A climate of success is established by furnishing the correct answers at the end of each test.

You soon learn to recognize types of questions, forms of questions, and patterns of questioning. You may even begin to anticipate expected outcomes.

You perceive that many questions are repeated or adapted so that you can gain acute insights, which may enable you to score many sure points.

You learn how to confront new questions, or types of questions, and to attack them confidently and work out the correct answers.

You note objectives and emphases, and recognize pitfalls and dangers, so that you may make positive educational adjustments.

Moreover, you are kept fully informed in relation to new concepts, methods, practices, and directions in the field.

You discover that you are actually taking the examination all the time: you are preparing for the examination by "taking" an examination, not by reading extraneous and/or supererogatory textbooks.

In short, this PASSBOOK®, used directedly, should be an important factor in helping you to pass your test.

INVESTIGATOR

DUTIES:
As an Investigator, you would conduct field investigations of either reported or suspected violations of law, rule or regulation or of an individual's background in order to gather or verify information for the administration of an agency's enforcement, regulatory, compensation award or licensing program. Incumbents regularly question witnesses and complainants, review documents, and maintain surveillance of individuals/businesses to obtain information relative to the conduct of the investigation.

SCOPE OF THE EXAMINATION:
The multiple-choice written test will cover knowledge, skills and/or abilities in such areas as:
1. Evaluating information and evidence;
2. Investigative techniques;
3. Preparing written material; and
4. Understanding and interpreting written material.

HOW TO TAKE A TEST

I. YOU MUST PASS AN EXAMINATION

A. *WHAT EVERY CANDIDATE SHOULD KNOW*

Examination applicants often ask us for help in preparing for the written test. What can I study in advance? What kinds of questions will be asked? How will the test be given? How will the papers be graded?

As an applicant for a civil service examination, you may be wondering about some of these things. Our purpose here is to suggest effective methods of advance study and to describe civil service examinations.

Your chances for success on this examination can be increased if you know how to prepare. Those "pre-examination jitters" can be reduced if you know what to expect. You can even experience an adventure in good citizenship if you know why civil service exams are given.

B. *WHY ARE CIVIL SERVICE EXAMINATIONS GIVEN?*

Civil service examinations are important to you in two ways. As a citizen, you want public jobs filled by employees who know how to do their work. As a job seeker, you want a fair chance to compete for that job on an equal footing with other candidates. The best-known means of accomplishing this two-fold goal is the competitive examination.

Exams are widely publicized throughout the nation. They may be administered for jobs in federal, state, city, municipal, town or village governments or agencies.

Any citizen may apply, with some limitations, such as the age or residence of applicants. Your experience and education may be reviewed to see whether you meet the requirements for the particular examination. When these requirements exist, they are reasonable and applied consistently to all applicants. Thus, a competitive examination may cause you some uneasiness now, but it is your privilege and safeguard.

C. *HOW ARE CIVIL SERVICE EXAMS DEVELOPED?*

Examinations are carefully written by trained technicians who are specialists in the field known as "psychological measurement," in consultation with recognized authorities in the field of work that the test will cover. These experts recommend the subject matter areas or skills to be tested; only those knowledges or skills important to your success on the job are included. The most reliable books and source materials available are used as references. Together, the experts and technicians judge the difficulty level of the questions.

Test technicians know how to phrase questions so that the problem is clearly stated. Their ethics do not permit "trick" or "catch" questions. Questions may have been tried out on sample groups, or subjected to statistical analysis, to determine their usefulness.

Written tests are often used in combination with performance tests, ratings of training and experience, and oral interviews. All of these measures combine to form the best-known means of finding the right person for the right job.

II. HOW TO PASS THE WRITTEN TEST

A. NATURE OF THE EXAMINATION

To prepare intelligently for civil service examinations, you should know how they differ from school examinations you have taken. In school you were assigned certain definite pages to read or subjects to cover. The examination questions were quite detailed and usually emphasized memory. Civil service exams, on the other hand, try to discover your present ability to perform the duties of a position, plus your potentiality to learn these duties. In other words, a civil service exam attempts to predict how successful you will be. Questions cover such a broad area that they cannot be as minute and detailed as school exam questions.

In the public service similar kinds of work, or positions, are grouped together in one "class." This process is known as *position-classification*. All the positions in a class are paid according to the salary range for that class. One class title covers all of these positions, and they are all tested by the same examination.

B. FOUR BASIC STEPS

1) Study the announcement

How, then, can you know what subjects to study? Our best answer is: "Learn as much as possible about the class of positions for which you've applied." The exam will test the knowledge, skills and abilities needed to do the work.

Your most valuable source of information about the position you want is the official exam announcement. This announcement lists the training and experience qualifications. Check these standards and apply only if you come reasonably close to meeting them.

The brief description of the position in the examination announcement offers some clues to the subjects which will be tested. Think about the job itself. Review the duties in your mind. Can you perform them, or are there some in which you are rusty? Fill in the blank spots in your preparation.

Many jurisdictions preview the written test in the exam announcement by including a section called "Knowledge and Abilities Required," "Scope of the Examination," or some similar heading. Here you will find out specifically what fields will be tested.

2) Review your own background

Once you learn in general what the position is all about, and what you need to know to do the work, ask yourself which subjects you already know fairly well and which need improvement. You may wonder whether to concentrate on improving your strong areas or on building some background in your fields of weakness. When the announcement has specified "some knowledge" or "considerable knowledge," or has used adjectives like "beginning principles of…" or "advanced … methods," you can get a clue as to the number and difficulty of questions to be asked in any given field. More questions, and hence broader coverage, would be included for those subjects which are more important in the work. Now weigh your strengths and weaknesses against the job requirements and prepare accordingly.

3) Determine the level of the position

Another way to tell how intensively you should prepare is to understand the level of the job for which you are applying. Is it the entering level? In other words, is this the position in which beginners in a field of work are hired? Or is it an intermediate or advanced level? Sometimes this is indicated by such words as "Junior" or "Senior" in the class title. Other jurisdictions use Roman numerals to designate the level – Clerk I, Clerk II, for example. The word "Supervisor" sometimes appears in the title. If the level is not indicated by the title, check the description of duties. Will you be working under very close supervision, or will you have responsibility for independent decisions in this work?

4) Choose appropriate study materials

Now that you know the subjects to be examined and the relative amount of each subject to be covered, you can choose suitable study materials. For beginning level jobs, or even advanced ones, if you have a pronounced weakness in some aspect of your training, read a modern, standard textbook in that field. Be sure it is up to date and has general coverage. Such books are normally available at your library, and the librarian will be glad to help you locate one. For entry-level positions, questions of appropriate difficulty are chosen – neither highly advanced questions, nor those too simple. Such questions require careful thought but not advanced training.

If the position for which you are applying is technical or advanced, you will read more advanced, specialized material. If you are already familiar with the basic principles of your field, elementary textbooks would waste your time. Concentrate on advanced textbooks and technical periodicals. Think through the concepts and review difficult problems in your field.

These are all general sources. You can get more ideas on your own initiative, following these leads. For example, training manuals and publications of the government agency which employs workers in your field can be useful, particularly for technical and professional positions. A letter or visit to the government department involved may result in more specific study suggestions, and certainly will provide you with a more definite idea of the exact nature of the position you are seeking.

III. KINDS OF TESTS

Tests are used for purposes other than measuring knowledge and ability to perform specified duties. For some positions, it is equally important to test ability to make adjustments to new situations or to profit from training. In others, basic mental abilities not dependent on information are essential. Questions which test these things may not appear as pertinent to the duties of the position as those which test for knowledge and information. Yet they are often highly important parts of a fair examination. For very general questions, it is almost impossible to help you direct your study efforts. What we can do is to point out some of the more common of these general abilities needed in public service positions and describe some typical questions.

1) General information

Broad, general information has been found useful for predicting job success in some kinds of work. This is tested in a variety of ways, from vocabulary lists to questions about current events. Basic background in some field of work, such as sociology or economics, may be sampled in a group of questions. Often these are principles which have become familiar to most persons through exposure rather than through formal training. It is difficult to advise you how to study for these questions; being alert to the world around you is our best suggestion.

2) Verbal ability

An example of an ability needed in many positions is verbal or language ability. Verbal ability is, in brief, the ability to use and understand words. Vocabulary and grammar tests are typical measures of this ability. Reading comprehension or paragraph interpretation questions are common in many kinds of civil service tests. You are given a paragraph of written material and asked to find its central meaning.

3) Numerical ability

Number skills can be tested by the familiar arithmetic problem, by checking paired lists of numbers to see which are alike and which are different, or by interpreting charts and graphs. In the latter test, a graph may be printed in the test booklet which you are asked to use as the basis for answering questions.

4) Observation

A popular test for law-enforcement positions is the observation test. A picture is shown to you for several minutes, then taken away. Questions about the picture test your ability to observe both details and larger elements.

5) Following directions

In many positions in the public service, the employee must be able to carry out written instructions dependably and accurately. You may be given a chart with several columns, each column listing a variety of information. The questions require you to carry out directions involving the information given in the chart.

6) Skills and aptitudes

Performance tests effectively measure some manual skills and aptitudes. When the skill is one in which you are trained, such as typing or shorthand, you can practice. These tests are often very much like those given in business school or high school courses. For many of the other skills and aptitudes, however, no short-time preparation can be made. Skills and abilities natural to you or that you have developed throughout your lifetime are being tested.

Many of the general questions just described provide all the data needed to answer the questions and ask you to use your reasoning ability to find the answers. Your best preparation for these tests, as well as for tests of facts and ideas, is to be at your physical and mental best. You, no doubt, have your own methods of getting into an exam-taking mood and keeping "in shape." The next section lists some ideas on this subject.

IV. KINDS OF QUESTIONS

Only rarely is the "essay" question, which you answer in narrative form, used in civil service tests. Civil service tests are usually of the short-answer type. Full instructions for answering these questions will be given to you at the examination. But in case this is your first experience with short-answer questions and separate answer sheets, here is what you need to know:

1) Multiple-choice Questions

Most popular of the short-answer questions is the "multiple choice" or "best answer" question. It can be used, for example, to test for factual knowledge, ability to solve problems or judgment in meeting situations found at work.

A multiple-choice question is normally one of three types—
- It can begin with an incomplete statement followed by several possible endings. You are to find the one ending which *best* completes the statement, although some of the others may not be entirely wrong.
- It can also be a complete statement in the form of a question which is answered by choosing one of the statements listed.

- It can be in the form of a problem – again you select the best answer.

Here is an example of a multiple-choice question with a discussion which should give you some clues as to the method for choosing the right answer:

When an employee has a complaint about his assignment, the action which will *best* help him overcome his difficulty is to
- A. discuss his difficulty with his coworkers
- B. take the problem to the head of the organization
- C. take the problem to the person who gave him the assignment
- D. say nothing to anyone about his complaint

In answering this question, you should study each of the choices to find which is best. Consider choice "A" – Certainly an employee may discuss his complaint with fellow employees, but no change or improvement can result, and the complaint remains unresolved. Choice "B" is a poor choice since the head of the organization probably does not know what assignment you have been given, and taking your problem to him is known as "going over the head" of the supervisor. The supervisor, or person who made the assignment, is the person who can clarify it or correct any injustice. Choice "C" is, therefore, correct. To say nothing, as in choice "D," is unwise. Supervisors have and interest in knowing the problems employees are facing, and the employee is seeking a solution to his problem.

2) True/False Questions

The "true/false" or "right/wrong" form of question is sometimes used. Here a complete statement is given. Your job is to decide whether the statement is right or wrong.

SAMPLE: A roaming cell-phone call to a nearby city costs less than a non-roaming call to a distant city.

This statement is wrong, or false, since roaming calls are more expensive.
This is not a complete list of all possible question forms, although most of the others are variations of these common types. You will always get complete directions for answering questions. Be sure you understand *how* to mark your answers – ask questions until you do.

V. RECORDING YOUR ANSWERS

Computer terminals are used more and more today for many different kinds of exams.
For an examination with very few applicants, you may be told to record your answers in the test booklet itself. Separate answer sheets are much more common. If this separate answer sheet is to be scored by machine – and this is often the case – it is highly important that you mark your answers correctly in order to get credit.
An electronic scoring machine is often used in civil service offices because of the speed with which papers can be scored. Machine-scored answer sheets must be marked with a pencil, which will be given to you. This pencil has a high graphite content which responds to the electronic scoring machine. As a matter of fact, stray dots may register as answers, so do not let your pencil rest on the answer sheet while you are pondering the correct answer. Also, if your pencil lead breaks or is otherwise defective, ask for another.

Since the answer sheet will be dropped in a slot in the scoring machine, be careful not to bend the corners or get the paper crumpled.

The answer sheet normally has five vertical columns of numbers, with 30 numbers to a column. These numbers correspond to the question numbers in your test booklet. After each number, going across the page are four or five pairs of dotted lines. These short dotted lines have small letters or numbers above them. The first two pairs may also have a "T" or "F" above the letters. This indicates that the first two pairs only are to be used if the questions are of the true-false type. If the questions are multiple choice, disregard the "T" and "F" and pay attention only to the small letters or numbers.

Answer your questions in the manner of the sample that follows:

32. The largest city in the United States is
    A. Washington, D.C.
    B. New York City
    C. Chicago
    D. Detroit
    E. San Francisco

1) Choose the answer you think is best. (New York City is the largest, so "B" is correct.)
2) Find the row of dotted lines numbered the same as the question you are answering. (Find row number 32)
3) Find the pair of dotted lines corresponding to the answer. (Find the pair of lines under the mark "B.")
4) Make a solid black mark between the dotted lines.

VI. BEFORE THE TEST

Common sense will help you find procedures to follow to get ready for an examination. Too many of us, however, overlook these sensible measures. Indeed, nervousness and fatigue have been found to be the most serious reasons why applicants fail to do their best on civil service tests. Here is a list of reminders:

- Begin your preparation early – Don't wait until the last minute to go scurrying around for books and materials or to find out what the position is all about.
- Prepare continuously – An hour a night for a week is better than an all-night cram session. This has been definitely established. What is more, a night a week for a month will return better dividends than crowding your study into a shorter period of time.
- Locate the place of the exam – You have been sent a notice telling you when and where to report for the examination. If the location is in a different town or otherwise unfamiliar to you, it would be well to inquire the best route and learn something about the building.
- Relax the night before the test – Allow your mind to rest. Do not study at all that night. Plan some mild recreation or diversion; then go to bed early and get a good night's sleep.
- Get up early enough to make a leisurely trip to the place for the test – This way unforeseen events, traffic snarls, unfamiliar buildings, etc. will not upset you.
- Dress comfortably – A written test is not a fashion show. You will be known by number and not by name, so wear something comfortable.

- Leave excess paraphernalia at home – Shopping bags and odd bundles will get in your way. You need bring only the items mentioned in the official notice you received; usually everything you need is provided. Do not bring reference books to the exam. They will only confuse those last minutes and be taken away from you when in the test room.
- Arrive somewhat ahead of time – If because of transportation schedules you must get there very early, bring a newspaper or magazine to take your mind off yourself while waiting.
- Locate the examination room – When you have found the proper room, you will be directed to the seat or part of the room where you will sit. Sometimes you are given a sheet of instructions to read while you are waiting. Do not fill out any forms until you are told to do so; just read them and be prepared.
- Relax and prepare to listen to the instructions
- If you have any physical problem that may keep you from doing your best, be sure to tell the test administrator. If you are sick or in poor health, you really cannot do your best on the exam. You can come back and take the test some other time.

VII. AT THE TEST

The day of the test is here and you have the test booklet in your hand. The temptation to get going is very strong. Caution! There is more to success than knowing the right answers. You must know how to identify your papers and understand variations in the type of short-answer question used in this particular examination. Follow these suggestions for maximum results from your efforts:

1) Cooperate with the monitor

The test administrator has a duty to create a situation in which you can be as much at ease as possible. He will give instructions, tell you when to begin, check to see that you are marking your answer sheet correctly, and so on. He is not there to guard you, although he will see that your competitors do not take unfair advantage. He wants to help you do your best.

2) Listen to all instructions

Don't jump the gun! Wait until you understand all directions. In most civil service tests you get more time than you need to answer the questions. So don't be in a hurry. Read each word of instructions until you clearly understand the meaning. Study the examples, listen to all announcements and follow directions. Ask questions if you do not understand what to do.

3) Identify your papers

Civil service exams are usually identified by number only. You will be assigned a number; you must not put your name on your test papers. Be sure to copy your number correctly. Since more than one exam may be given, copy your exact examination title.

4) Plan your time

Unless you are told that a test is a "speed" or "rate of work" test, speed itself is usually not important. Time enough to answer all the questions will be provided, but this does not mean that you have all day. An overall time limit has been set. Divide the total time (in minutes) by the number of questions to determine the approximate time you have for each question.

5) Do not linger over difficult questions

If you come across a difficult question, mark it with a paper clip (useful to have along) and come back to it when you have been through the booklet. One caution if you do this – be sure to skip a number on your answer sheet as well. Check often to be sure that you have not lost your place and that you are marking in the row numbered the same as the question you are answering.

6) Read the questions

Be sure you know what the question asks! Many capable people are unsuccessful because they failed to *read* the questions correctly.

7) Answer all questions

Unless you have been instructed that a penalty will be deducted for incorrect answers, it is better to guess than to omit a question.

8) Speed tests

It is often better NOT to guess on speed tests. It has been found that on timed tests people are tempted to spend the last few seconds before time is called in marking answers at random – without even reading them – in the hope of picking up a few extra points. To discourage this practice, the instructions may warn you that your score will be "corrected" for guessing. That is, a penalty will be applied. The incorrect answers will be deducted from the correct ones, or some other penalty formula will be used.

9) Review your answers

If you finish before time is called, go back to the questions you guessed or omitted to give them further thought. Review other answers if you have time.

10) Return your test materials

If you are ready to leave before others have finished or time is called, take ALL your materials to the monitor and leave quietly. Never take any test material with you. The monitor can discover whose papers are not complete, and taking a test booklet may be grounds for disqualification.

VIII. EXAMINATION TECHNIQUES

1) Read the general instructions carefully. These are usually printed on the first page of the exam booklet. As a rule, these instructions refer to the timing of the examination; the fact that you should not start work until the signal and must stop work at a signal, etc. If there are any *special* instructions, such as a choice of questions to be answered, make sure that you note this instruction carefully.

2) When you are ready to start work on the examination, that is as soon as the signal has been given, read the instructions to each question booklet, underline any key words or phrases, such as *least, best, outline, describe* and the like. In this way you will tend to answer as requested rather than discover on reviewing your paper that you *listed without describing*, that you selected the *worst* choice rather than the *best* choice, etc.

3) If the examination is of the objective or multiple-choice type – that is, each question will also give a series of possible answers: A, B, C or D, and you are called upon to select the best answer and write the letter next to that answer on your answer paper – it is advisable to start answering each question in turn. There may be anywhere from 50 to 100 such questions in the three or four hours allotted and you can see how much time would be taken if you read through all the questions before beginning to answer any. Furthermore, if you come across a question or group of questions which you know would be difficult to answer, it would undoubtedly affect your handling of all the other questions.

4) If the examination is of the essay type and contains but a few questions, it is a moot point as to whether you should read all the questions before starting to answer any one. Of course, if you are given a choice – say five out of seven and the like – then it is essential to read all the questions so you can eliminate the two that are most difficult. If, however, you are asked to answer all the questions, there may be danger in trying to answer the easiest one first because you may find that you will spend too much time on it. The best technique is to answer the first question, then proceed to the second, etc.

5) Time your answers. Before the exam begins, write down the time it started, then add the time allowed for the examination and write down the time it must be completed, then divide the time available somewhat as follows:
   - If 3-1/2 hours are allowed, that would be 210 minutes. If you have 80 objective-type questions, that would be an average of 2-1/2 minutes per question. Allow yourself no more than 2 minutes per question, or a total of 160 minutes, which will permit about 50 minutes to review.
   - If for the time allotment of 210 minutes there are 7 essay questions to answer, that would average about 30 minutes a question. Give yourself only 25 minutes per question so that you have about 35 minutes to review.

6) The most important instruction is to *read each question* and make sure you know what is wanted. The second most important instruction is to *time yourself properly* so that you answer every question. The third most important instruction is to *answer every question*. Guess if you have to but include something for each question. Remember that you will receive no credit for a blank and will probably receive some credit if you write something in answer to an essay question. If you guess a letter – say "B" for a multiple-choice question – you may have guessed right. If you leave a blank as an answer to a multiple-choice question, the examiners may respect your feelings but it will not add a point to your score. Some exams may penalize you for wrong answers, so in such cases *only*, you may not want to guess unless you have some basis for your answer.

7) Suggestions
   a. Objective-type questions
      1. Examine the question booklet for proper sequence of pages and questions
      2. Read all instructions carefully
      3. Skip any question which seems too difficult; return to it after all other questions have been answered
      4. Apportion your time properly; do not spend too much time on any single question or group of questions

5. Note and underline key words – *all, most, fewest, least, best, worst, same, opposite,* etc.
6. Pay particular attention to negatives
7. Note unusual option, e.g., unduly long, short, complex, different or similar in content to the body of the question
8. Observe the use of "hedging" words – *probably, may, most likely,* etc.
9. Make sure that your answer is put next to the same number as the question
10. Do not second-guess unless you have good reason to believe the second answer is definitely more correct
11. Cross out original answer if you decide another answer is more accurate; do not erase until you are ready to hand your paper in
12. Answer all questions; guess unless instructed otherwise
13. Leave time for review

   b. Essay questions
      1. Read each question carefully
      2. Determine exactly what is wanted. Underline key words or phrases.
      3. Decide on outline or paragraph answer
      4. Include many different points and elements unless asked to develop any one or two points or elements
      5. Show impartiality by giving pros and cons unless directed to select one side only
      6. Make and write down any assumptions you find necessary to answer the questions
      7. Watch your English, grammar, punctuation and choice of words
      8. Time your answers; don't crowd material

8) Answering the essay question

Most essay questions can be answered by framing the specific response around several key words or ideas. Here are a few such key words or ideas:

M's: manpower, materials, methods, money, management
P's: purpose, program, policy, plan, procedure, practice, problems, pitfalls, personnel, public relations

   a. Six basic steps in handling problems:
      1. Preliminary plan and background development
      2. Collect information, data and facts
      3. Analyze and interpret information, data and facts
      4. Analyze and develop solutions as well as make recommendations
      5. Prepare report and sell recommendations
      6. Install recommendations and follow up effectiveness

   b. Pitfalls to avoid
      1. *Taking things for granted* – A statement of the situation does not necessarily imply that each of the elements is necessarily true; for example, a complaint may be invalid and biased so that all that can be taken for granted is that a complaint has been registered

2. *Considering only one side of a situation* – Wherever possible, indicate several alternatives and then point out the reasons you selected the best one
3. *Failing to indicate follow up* – Whenever your answer indicates action on your part, make certain that you will take proper follow-up action to see how successful your recommendations, procedures or actions turn out to be
4. *Taking too long in answering any single question* – Remember to time your answers properly

IX. AFTER THE TEST

Scoring procedures differ in detail among civil service jurisdictions although the general principles are the same. Whether the papers are hand-scored or graded by machine we have described, they are nearly always graded by number. That is, the person who marks the paper knows only the number – never the name – of the applicant. Not until all the papers have been graded will they be matched with names. If other tests, such as training and experience or oral interview ratings have been given, scores will be combined. Different parts of the examination usually have different weights. For example, the written test might count 60 percent of the final grade, and a rating of training and experience 40 percent. In many jurisdictions, veterans will have a certain number of points added to their grades.

After the final grade has been determined, the names are placed in grade order and an eligible list is established. There are various methods for resolving ties between those who get the same final grade – probably the most common is to place first the name of the person whose application was received first. Job offers are made from the eligible list in the order the names appear on it. You will be notified of your grade and your rank as soon as all these computations have been made. This will be done as rapidly as possible.

People who are found to meet the requirements in the announcement are called "eligibles." Their names are put on a list of eligible candidates. An eligible's chances of getting a job depend on how high he stands on this list and how fast agencies are filling jobs from the list.

When a job is to be filled from a list of eligibles, the agency asks for the names of people on the list of eligibles for that job. When the civil service commission receives this request, it sends to the agency the names of the three people highest on this list. Or, if the job to be filled has specialized requirements, the office sends the agency the names of the top three persons who meet these requirements from the general list.

The appointing officer makes a choice from among the three people whose names were sent to him. If the selected person accepts the appointment, the names of the others are put back on the list to be considered for future openings.

That is the rule in hiring from all kinds of eligible lists, whether they are for typist, carpenter, chemist, or something else. For every vacancy, the appointing officer has his choice of any one of the top three eligibles on the list. This explains why the person whose name is on top of the list sometimes does not get an appointment when some of the persons lower on the list do. If the appointing officer chooses the second or third eligible, the No. 1 eligible does not get a job at once, but stays on the list until he is appointed or the list is terminated.

X. HOW TO PASS THE INTERVIEW TEST

The examination for which you applied requires an oral interview test. You have already taken the written test and you are now being called for the interview test – the final part of the formal examination.

You may think that it is not possible to prepare for an interview test and that there are no procedures to follow during an interview. Our purpose is to point out some things you can do in advance that will help you and some good rules to follow and pitfalls to avoid while you are being interviewed.

What is an interview supposed to test?

The written examination is designed to test the technical knowledge and competence of the candidate; the oral is designed to evaluate intangible qualities, not readily measured otherwise, and to establish a list showing the relative fitness of each candidate – as measured against his competitors – for the position sought. Scoring is not on the basis of "right" and "wrong," but on a sliding scale of values ranging from "not passable" to "outstanding." As a matter of fact, it is possible to achieve a relatively low score without a single "incorrect" answer because of evident weakness in the qualities being measured.

Occasionally, an examination may consist entirely of an oral test – either an individual or a group oral. In such cases, information is sought concerning the technical knowledges and abilities of the candidate, since there has been no written examination for this purpose. More commonly, however, an oral test is used to supplement a written examination.

Who conducts interviews?

The composition of oral boards varies among different jurisdictions. In nearly all, a representative of the personnel department serves as chairman. One of the members of the board may be a representative of the department in which the candidate would work. In some cases, "outside experts" are used, and, frequently, a businessman or some other representative of the general public is asked to serve. Labor and management or other special groups may be represented. The aim is to secure the services of experts in the appropriate field.

However the board is composed, it is a good idea (and not at all improper or unethical) to ascertain in advance of the interview who the members are and what groups they represent. When you are introduced to them, you will have some idea of their backgrounds and interests, and at least you will not stutter and stammer over their names.

What should be done before the interview?

While knowledge about the board members is useful and takes some of the surprise element out of the interview, there is other preparation which is more substantive. It *is* possible to prepare for an oral interview – in several ways:

1) Keep a copy of your application and review it carefully before the interview

This may be the only document before the oral board, and the starting point of the interview. Know what education and experience you have listed there, and the sequence and dates of all of it. Sometimes the board will ask you to review the highlights of your experience for them; you should not have to hem and haw doing it.

2) Study the class specification and the examination announcement

Usually, the oral board has one or both of these to guide them. The qualities, characteristics or knowledges required by the position sought are stated in these documents. They offer valuable clues as to the nature of the oral interview. For example, if the job involves supervisory responsibilities, the announcement will usually indicate that knowledge of modern supervisory methods and the qualifications of the candidate as a supervisor will be tested. If so, you can expect such questions, frequently in the form of a hypothetical situation which you are expected to solve. NEVER go into an oral without knowledge of the duties and responsibilities of the job you seek.

3) Think through each qualification required

Try to visualize the kind of questions you would ask if you were a board member. How well could you answer them? Try especially to appraise your own knowledge and background in each area, *measured against the job sought*, and identify any areas in which you are weak. Be critical and realistic – do not flatter yourself.

4) Do some general reading in areas in which you feel you may be weak

For example, if the job involves supervision and your past experience has NOT, some general reading in supervisory methods and practices, particularly in the field of human relations, might be useful. Do NOT study agency procedures or detailed manuals. The oral board will be testing your understanding and capacity, not your memory.

5) Get a good night's sleep and watch your general health and mental attitude

You will want a clear head at the interview. Take care of a cold or any other minor ailment, and of course, no hangovers.

What should be done on the day of the interview?

Now comes the day of the interview itself. Give yourself plenty of time to get there. Plan to arrive somewhat ahead of the scheduled time, particularly if your appointment is in the fore part of the day. If a previous candidate fails to appear, the board might be ready for you a bit early. By early afternoon an oral board is almost invariably behind schedule if there are many candidates, and you may have to wait. Take along a book or magazine to read, or your application to review, but leave any extraneous material in the waiting room when you go in for your interview. In any event, relax and compose yourself.

The matter of dress is important. The board is forming impressions about you – from your experience, your manners, your attitude, and your appearance. Give your personal appearance careful attention. Dress your best, but not your flashiest. Choose conservative, appropriate clothing, and be sure it is immaculate. This is a business interview, and your appearance should indicate that you regard it as such. Besides, being well groomed and properly dressed will help boost your confidence.

Sooner or later, someone will call your name and escort you into the interview room. *This is it.* From here on you are on your own. It is too late for any more preparation. But remember, you asked for this opportunity to prove your fitness, and you are here because your request was granted.

What happens when you go in?

The usual sequence of events will be as follows: The clerk (who is often the board stenographer) will introduce you to the chairman of the oral board, who will introduce you to the other members of the board. Acknowledge the introductions before you sit down. Do not be surprised if you find a microphone facing you or a stenotypist sitting by. Oral interviews are usually recorded in the event of an appeal or other review.

Usually the chairman of the board will open the interview by reviewing the highlights of your education and work experience from your application – primarily for the benefit of the other members of the board, as well as to get the material into the record. Do not interrupt or comment unless there is an error or significant misinterpretation; if that is the case, do not hesitate. But do not quibble about insignificant matters. Also, he will usually ask you some question about your education, experience or your present job – partly to get you to start talking and to establish the interviewing "rapport." He may start the actual questioning, or turn it over to one of the other members. Frequently, each member undertakes the questioning on a particular area, one in which he is perhaps most competent, so you can expect each member to participate in the examination. Because time is limited, you may also expect some rather abrupt switches in the direction the questioning takes, so do not be upset by it. Normally, a board member will not pursue a single line of questioning unless he discovers a particular strength or weakness.

After each member has participated, the chairman will usually ask whether any member has any further questions, then will ask you if you have anything you wish to add. Unless you are expecting this question, it may floor you. Worse, it may start you off on an extended, extemporaneous speech. The board is not usually seeking more information. The question is principally to offer you a last opportunity to present further qualifications or to indicate that you have nothing to add. So, if you feel that a significant qualification or characteristic has been overlooked, it is proper to point it out in a sentence or so. Do not compliment the board on the thoroughness of their examination – they have been sketchy, and you know it. If you wish, merely say, "No thank you, I have nothing further to add." This is a point where you can "talk yourself out" of a good impression or fail to present an important bit of information. Remember, *you close the interview yourself*.

The chairman will then say, "That is all, Mr. _____, thank you." Do not be startled; the interview is over, and quicker than you think. Thank him, gather your belongings and take your leave. Save your sigh of relief for the other side of the door.

How to put your best foot forward

Throughout this entire process, you may feel that the board individually and collectively is trying to pierce your defenses, seek out your hidden weaknesses and embarrass and confuse you. Actually, this is not true. They are obliged to make an appraisal of your qualifications for the job you are seeking, and they want to see you in your best light. Remember, they must interview all candidates and a non-cooperative candidate may become a failure in spite of their best efforts to bring out his qualifications. Here are 15 suggestions that will help you:

1) Be natural – Keep your attitude confident, not cocky

If you are not confident that you can do the job, do not expect the board to be. Do not apologize for your weaknesses, try to bring out your strong points. The board is interested in a positive, not negative, presentation. Cockiness will antagonize any board member and make him wonder if you are covering up a weakness by a false show of strength.

2) Get comfortable, but don't lounge or sprawl

Sit erectly but not stiffly. A careless posture may lead the board to conclude that you are careless in other things, or at least that you are not impressed by the importance of the occasion. Either conclusion is natural, even if incorrect. Do not fuss with your clothing, a pencil or an ashtray. Your hands may occasionally be useful to emphasize a point; do not let them become a point of distraction.

3) Do not wisecrack or make small talk

This is a serious situation, and your attitude should show that you consider it as such. Further, the time of the board is limited – they do not want to waste it, and neither should you.

4) Do not exaggerate your experience or abilities
In the first place, from information in the application or other interviews and sources, the board may know more about you than you think. Secondly, you probably will not get away with it. An experienced board is rather adept at spotting such a situation, so do not take the chance.

5) If you know a board member, do not make a point of it, yet do not hide it
Certainly you are not fooling him, and probably not the other members of the board. Do not try to take advantage of your acquaintanceship – it will probably do you little good.

6) Do not dominate the interview
Let the board do that. They will give you the clues – do not assume that you have to do all the talking. Realize that the board has a number of questions to ask you, and do not try to take up all the interview time by showing off your extensive knowledge of the answer to the first one.

7) Be attentive
You only have 20 minutes or so, and you should keep your attention at its sharpest throughout. When a member is addressing a problem or question to you, give him your undivided attention. Address your reply principally to him, but do not exclude the other board members.

8) Do not interrupt
A board member may be stating a problem for you to analyze. He will ask you a question when the time comes. Let him state the problem, and wait for the question.

9) Make sure you understand the question
Do not try to answer until you are sure what the question is. If it is not clear, restate it in your own words or ask the board member to clarify it for you. However, do not haggle about minor elements.

10) Reply promptly but not hastily
A common entry on oral board rating sheets is "candidate responded readily," or "candidate hesitated in replies." Respond as promptly and quickly as you can, but do not jump to a hasty, ill-considered answer.

11) Do not be peremptory in your answers
A brief answer is proper – but do not fire your answer back. That is a losing game from your point of view. The board member can probably ask questions much faster than you can answer them.

12) Do not try to create the answer you think the board member wants
He is interested in what kind of mind you have and how it works – not in playing games. Furthermore, he can usually spot this practice and will actually grade you down on it.

13) Do not switch sides in your reply merely to agree with a board member
Frequently, a member will take a contrary position merely to draw you out and to see if you are willing and able to defend your point of view. Do not start a debate, yet do not surrender a good position. If a position is worth taking, it is worth defending.

14) Do not be afraid to admit an error in judgment if you are shown to be wrong

The board knows that you are forced to reply without any opportunity for careful consideration. Your answer may be demonstrably wrong. If so, admit it and get on with the interview.

15) Do not dwell at length on your present job

The opening question may relate to your present assignment. Answer the question but do not go into an extended discussion. You are being examined for a *new* job, not your present one. As a matter of fact, try to phrase ALL your answers in terms of the job for which you are being examined.

Basis of Rating

Probably you will forget most of these "do's" and "don'ts" when you walk into the oral interview room. Even remembering them all will not ensure you a passing grade. Perhaps you did not have the qualifications in the first place. But remembering them will help you to put your best foot forward, without treading on the toes of the board members.

Rumor and popular opinion to the contrary notwithstanding, an oral board wants you to make the best appearance possible. They know you are under pressure – but they also want to see how you respond to it as a guide to what your reaction would be under the pressures of the job you seek. They will be influenced by the degree of poise you display, the personal traits you show and the manner in which you respond.

ABOUT THIS BOOK

This book contains tests divided into Examination Sections. Go through each test, answering every question in the margin. We have also attached a sample answer sheet at the back of the book that can be removed and used. At the end of each test look at the answer key and check your answers. On the ones you got wrong, look at the right answer choice and learn. Do not fill in the answers first. Do not memorize the questions and answers, but understand the answer and principles involved. On your test, the questions will likely be different from the samples. Questions are changed and new ones added. If you understand these past questions you should have success with any changes that arise. Tests may consist of several types of questions. We have additional books on each subject should more study be advisable or necessary for you. Finally, the more you study, the better prepared you will be. This book is intended to be the last thing you study before you walk into the examination room. Prior study of relevant texts is also recommended. NLC publishes some of these in our Fundamental Series. Knowledge and good sense are important factors in passing your exam. Good luck also helps. So now study this Passbook, absorb the material contained within and take that knowledge into the examination. Then do your best to pass that exam.

EXAMINATION SECTION

EXAMINATION SECTION
TEST 1

DIRECTIONS: Each question or incomplete statement is followed by several suggested answers or completions. Select the one that BEST answers the question or completes the statement. *PRINT THE LETTER OF THE CORRECT ANSWER IN THE SPACE AT THE RIGHT.*

1. The one of the following which is the BEST description of a properly objective investigator is one who
    A. is friendly and sensitive to the client's feelings, without becoming emotionally involved
    B. is distant and impersonal, remaining unaffected by what the client says
    C. lets personal emotions enter as far as the client's situation calls for them
    D. becomes emotionally involved with the client's situation but without showing involvement

   1.____

2. The one of the following which is MOST necessary for successfully interviewing a person who belongs to a culture different from that of the investigator is for the investigator to
    A. have some appreciation of the other culture
    B. ignore those cultural differences which lead to bias
    C. stay away from sensitive, touchy issues
    D. assume the mannerisms of people in the other culture

   2.____

3. In fact-finding interviews, it is generally assumed that the smaller the number of interviewees, the greater the increase of reliability with the addition of others. The PROPER number of interviewees need to insure the accuracy of information obtain generally depends upon the
    A. educational level of those interviewed
    B. number of people who have the required information
    C. directness of the questions asked
    D. variability of the information received

   3.____

4. The one of the following which is generally MOST likely to be accurately described in an interview by an interviewee is
    A. the presence of a large painting in the investigator's office
    B. the number of people in the investigator's waiting room
    C. space relations
    D. duration of time

   4.____

5. The one of the following which is generally the BEST course of action for an investigator to take when interviewing a person who is reluctant to tell what he knows about a matter under investigation is to
    A. be curt and abrupt, and threaten the person with the consequences of his withholding information

   5.____

B. be firm and severe, and pressure the person into telling the needed information
C. be patient and candid with the person being questioned about the investigation since doing otherwise is not ethical
D. give the person false information about the investigation so he will give the needed information without realizing its importance

6. It is often recommended that an investigator prepare in advance a list of questions or topics to be covered in an interview.
The MAIN reason for such a checklist is to
   A. allow investigations to be assigned to less efficient investigators
   B. eliminate a large amount of follow-up paperwork
   C. aid the investigator in remembering to cover all important documents
   D. aid the investigator in maintaining an objective distance from the person interviewed

7. Usually, the CHIEF advantage of a directive approach in an interview is that the
   A. investigator maintains control over the course of the interview
   B. person interviewed is more likely to be put at ease
   C. person interviewed is generally left free to direct the interview
   D. investigator will not suggest answers to the person interviewed

8. Usually, the CHIEF advantage of a non-directive approach by an investigator in conducting an interview is that the
   A. investigator generally conceals what he is looking for in the interview
   B. person interviewed is more likely to express his true feelings about the topic under discussion
   C. person interviewed is more likely to follow an idea introduced by the investigator
   D. investigator can keep the discussion limited to topics he believes to be relevant

9. The one of the following which is generally the LEAST likely to be accurate in a description of an event given to an investigator is a statement about
   A. the presence of an object
   B. the number of people, when their number is small
   C. locations of people
   D. duration of time

10. Assume that you, an investigator, are conducting a character investigation. In an interview, the one of the following character traits of the person being interviewed which can USUALLY be determined with a good degree of reliability is
    A. honesty
    B. dependability
    C. forcefulness
    D. perseverance

11. As an investigator, you have been assigned the task of obtaining a family's social history.
    The BEST place for you to interview members of the family while obtaining this social history would generally be in
    A. the family's home
    B. your agency's general offices
    C. the home of a friend of the family
    D. your own private office

12. You, an investigator, are checking someone's work history.
    The way for you to get the MOST reliable information from a previous employer is to
    A. send personal letters; the employer will respond to the personal attention
    B. send form letters; the employer will cooperate readily since little time or effort is asked of him
    C. arrange a personal interview; the employer may offer information he would not care to put in a letter or speak over the phone
    D. telephone; this method is as effective as a personal interview and is much more convenient

13. The effect that attestation, or the formal taking of an oath, has on witness testimony is to
    A. decrease accuracy, since a witness under oath is more nervous about what is said
    B. makes little difference, since the witness is not too swayed by an oath
    C. increase accuracy, since a witness under oath feels more responsibility for what is said
    D. eliminate inaccuracy unless there is deliberate perjury on the part of the witness

14. If an investigator obtains testimony from persons in interviews by means of interrogation or asking questions rather than by letting the person freely relate the testimony, what is said will GENERALLY be
    A. greater in range and less accurate
    B. greater in range and more accurate
    C. about the same in range and less accurate
    D. about the same in range and more accurate

15. Experienced investigators have learned to phrase their questions carefully in order to obtain the desired response.
    Of the following, the question which would usually elicit the MOST accurate answer is:
    A. "How old are you?"
    B. "What is your income?"
    C. "How are you today?"
    D. "What is your date of birth?"

16. The one of the following questions which would generally lead to the LEAST reliable answer is:
    A. "Did you see a wallet?"
    B. "Was the German Shepherd gray?"
    C. "Didn't you see the stop sign?"
    D. "Did you see the guard on duty?"

17. Some investigators may make a practice of observing details of the surroundings when interviewing in someone's home or office.
Such a practice is GENERALLY considered
    A. *undesirable*, mainly because such snooping is unwarranted, unethical invasion of privacy
    B. *undesirable*, mainly because useful information is rarely, if ever, gained this way
    C. *desirable*, mainly because useful insights into the character of the person interviewed may be gained
    D. *desirable*, mainly because it is impossible to evaluate a person adequately without such observation of his environment

18. The one of the following questions which MOST often lead to a reliable answer is:
    A. "Was his hair very dark?"
    B. "Wasn't there a clock on the wall?"
    C. "Was the automobile white or gray?"
    D. "Did you see a motorcycle?"

19. The one of the following which can MOST accurately be determined by an investigator by means of interviewing is
    A. a person's intelligence
    B. factual information about an event
    C. a person's aptitude for a specific task
    D. a person's perceptions of his own abilities

20. The one of the following which is MOST likely to help a person being interviewed feel at ease is for the investigator to
    A. let him start the conversation
    B. give him an abundance of time
    C. be relaxed himself
    D. open the interview by telling a joke

21. If the interviewee is to perceive some goal for himself in the interview and thus be motivated to participate in it, it is important that he clearly understands some of the aspects of the interview.
Of the following aspects, the one the interviewee needs LEAST to understand is
    A. the purpose of the interview
    B. the mechanics of interviewing
    C. the use made of the information he contributes
    D. what will be expected of him in the interview

22. As an investigator working on a project requiring inter-agency cooperation, you find that employees of an agency involved in the project are constantly making it difficult for you to obtain necessary information.
Of the following, the BEST action for you to take FIRST is to
    A. discuss the problem with your supervisor
    B. speak with your counterpart in the other agency

C. discuss the problem with the head of the uncooperative agency
D. contact the head of your agency

23. The investigator is justified in misleading the interviewee only when, in the investigator's judgment, this is clearly required by the problem being investigated.
Such a practice is
   A. *necessary*; there are times when complete honesty will impede a successful investigation
   B. *unnecessary*; such a tactic is unethical and should never be employed
   C. *necessary*; an investigator must be guided by success rather than ethical considerations in an investigation
   D. *unnecessary*; it is clearly doubtful whether such a practice will help the investigator conclude the investigation successfully

23.____

24. Assume that, in investigating a case of possible welfare fraud, it becomes necessary to hold an interview in the client's home in order to observe family interaction and conditions. Upon arriving, the investigator finds that the client's living room is noisy and crowded, with neighbors present and children running in and out.
Of the following, the BEST course of action for the investigator to take is to
   A. conduct the interview in the living room after telling the children to behave and asking the neighbors to leave
   B. tell the client that it is impossible to conduct the interview in the apartment and make an appointment for the next day in the investigators office
   C. suggest that they move from the living room into the kitchen where there is a table on which he can write
   D. try his best to conduct the interview in the noisy and crowded living room

24.____

25. You, an investigator, are giving testimony in court about a matter you have investigated. An attorney is questioning you in an abrasive, badgering way and, in an insulting manner, calls into doubt your ability as an investigator. You lose your temper and respond angrily, telling the attorney to stop harassing and insulting you.
Of the following, the BEST description of such a response is that it is generally
   A. *appropriate*; as a witness in court, you do not have to take insults from anybody, including an attorney
   B. *inappropriate*; losing your temper will show that you are weak and cannot be trusted as an investigator
   C. *appropriate*; a judge and jury will usually respect someone who responds strongly to unjust provocation
   D. *inappropriate*; such conduct is unprofessional and may unfavorably impress a judge and jury

25.____

KEY (CORRECT ANSWERS)

1.	A		11.	A
2.	A		12.	C
3.	D		13.	C
4.	A		14.	A
5.	C		15.	D
6.	C		16.	B
7.	A		17.	C
8.	B		18.	D
9.	D		19.	D
10.	C		20.	C

21. B
22. A
23. A
24. C
25. D

TEST 2

DIRECTIONS: Each question or incomplete statement is followed by several suggested answers or completions. Select the one that BEST answers the question or completes the statement. *PRINT THE LETTER OF THE CORRECT ANSWER IN THE SPACE AT THE RIGHT.*

1. An investigator may have problems in obtaining information from persons who have a history of mental disturbance CHIEFLY because such persons are
    A. usually highly unstable so that they cannot give a coherent account of anything they have experienced
    B. usually very withdrawn so that they generally are unwilling to talk to anyone they do not know well
    C. often normal in manner so that an investigator may be unaware that their condition may bias information they provide
    D. often violent and may try to attack an investigator who questions them intensively about a topic which is sensitive

    1.____

2. Empathy can be defined as the ability of one individual to respond sensitively and imaginatively to another's feelings.
   For an investigator to be empathetic during an interview is USUALLY
    A. *undesirable*, mainly because an investigator should never be influenced by the feelings of the one being interviewed
    B. *desirable*, mainly because an interview will not be productive unless the investigator takes the side of the person interviewed
    C. *undesirable*, mainly because empathy usually leads an investigator to be biased in favor of the person being interviewed
    D. *desirable*, mainly because this ability allows the investigator to direct his questions more effectively to the person interviewed

    2.____

3. Assume that an investigator must, in the course of an investigation, question several people who know each other.
   To gather them all in one group and question them together is GENERALLY
    A. *good practice*, since any inaccurate information offered by one person would be corrected by others in the group
    B. *poor practice*, since people in a group rarely pay adequate attention to questions
    C. *good practice*, since the investigator will save much time and effort in this way
    D. *poor practice*, since the presence of several people can inhibit an individual from speaking

    3.____

4. While conducting a character investigation of a potential employee, you, as an investigator, notice that most community members interviewed have negative opinions of the candidate.
   Of the following statements about the usefulness of community opinions in such a matter, the one which is LEAST accurate is that

    4.____

A. prudence should be exercised in evaluating information received in a community contact
B. a community investigation sometimes elicits gossip which may present an exaggerated picture
C. community opinion is reliable when used to assess an individual's character
D. opinions which cannot be supported by facts must be considered as such

5. An effective investigator should know that the one of the following which LEAST describes why there is a wide range of individual behavior in human relations is that
   A. socio-economic status influences human behavior
   B. physical characteristics do not influence human behavior
   C. education influences human behavior
   D. childhood experience influences human behavior

6. In your investigative unit, you discern a growing friction between two co-workers which is beginning to impede the work of the unit.
   Of the following, the approach you should FIRST adopt is to
   A. mediate the friction yourself; if unsuccessful, then inform your supervisor
   B. ignore the friction; although detrimental, it is beyond your authority to settle
   C. promptly discuss the friction and possible course of action with other members of your unit
   D. promptly inform your supervisor of the friction and let him handle the matter

7. In certain cases, in order that an investigation be conducted successfully, an investigator must have the cooperation of people in the community.
   The one of the following which BEST describes how an investigator may gain community cooperation in an investigation is by
   A. using persuasion
   B. using authority
   C. spending many hours in the community
   D. being friendly with community leaders

8. During a field investigation, an investigator encounters an uncooperative interviewee.
   Of the following, the FIRST thing the investigator should do in such a situation is to
   A. try various appeals to win the interviewee over to a cooperative attitude
   B. try to ascertain the reason for non-cooperation
   C. promise the interviewee that all data will be kept confidential
   D. alter his interviewing technique with the uncooperative interviewee

9. You, as an investigator, discover that an interviewee who was requested to bring with him specific documents for his initial employment interview has forgotten the documents.

Of the following, the BEST course of action to take is to
- A. give the person a reasonable amount of time to furnish the document
- B. tell the person you will let him know how much additional time he could receive
- C. mark the person disqualified for employment; he has failed to provide reasonably requested data on time
- D. mark the person provisionally qualified for employment; upon receipt of the documents, he will be permanently qualified

10. As an investigator checking interviewees' work experience, you realize that the person whom you are to interview is only marginally fluent in English and has, therefore, requested permission to bring a translator with him.
    Of the following, the BEST course of action is to inform the interviewee that
    - A. outside translators may not be used
    - B. only city translators may be used
    - C. state law requires fluency in English of all civil servants
    - D. he may be assisted in the interview by his translator

11. Assume that during the course of an interview, an investigator is verbally attacked by the person being interview.
    Of the following, it would be MOST advisable for the investigator to
    - A. answer back in a matter-of-fact manner
    - B. ask the person to apologize and discontinue the interview
    - C. ignore the attack but adjourn the interview to another day
    - D. use restraint and continue the interview

12. Assume that an investigator finds that the person he is interviewing has difficulty finishing his sentences and seems to be groping for words.
    In such a case, the BEST approach for the investigator to take is to
    - A. say what he thinks the person has in mind
    - B. proceed patiently without calling attention to the problem
    - C. ask the person why he finds it difficult to finish his sentence
    - D. interrupt the interview until the person feels more relaxed

13. The one of the following which BEST describes the effect of the sympathetic approach in interviewing on the interviewee is that it will
    - A. have no discernible effect on the interviewee
    - B. calm the interviewee
    - C. lead the interviewee to understate his problems
    - D. mislead the interviewee

14. The one of the following characteristics which is a PRIMARY requisite for a successful investigative interview is
    - A. total curiosity
    - B. total sympathy
    - C. complete attention
    - D. complete dedication

15. Assume that you, an investigator, become aware that one of your colleagues has a drinking problem which is affecting the operations of your unit.
Of the following, the action which you should take FIRST is to
    A. give your colleague time to resolve the problem himself
    B. discuss the problem with your colleague
    C. inform your supervisor of the problem
    D. not involve yourself in your colleague's problem

16. Assume that an Assistant District Attorney has asked you, the investigator of an alleged welfare fraud, to conduct a follow-up interview with a primary state witness.
The one of the following which is MOST important in arranging such an interview is to
    A. keep the witness cooperative
    B. conduct the matter in secret
    C. allow the witness to determine where and when the interview takes place
    D. conduct the interview as soon as possible to insure a strong case

17. Assume that an investigative unit has received a complex task requiring team work.
Of the following, the one which is LEAST essential to the operations of a team effort is
    A. a small group
    B. a leader
    C. regular interaction between team members
    D. separate office space for each team member

18. By examining a candidate's employment record, an investigator can determine many things about the candidate.
Of the following, the one which is LEAST apparent from an employment record is the candidate's
    A. character
    B. willingness to work
    C. capacity to get along with co-workers
    D. potential for advancing in civil service

19. Assume that you, an investigator, are conducting an investigative interview in which the person being interviewed is using the interview as a forum for venting his anti-civil service feelings.
Of the following, the FIRST thing that you should do is to
    A. agree with the person; perhaps that will shorten the outburst
    B. respectfully disagree with the person; the decorum of the interview has already been disrupted
    C. courteously and objectively direct the interview to the relevant issue
    D. reschedule the interview to another mutually agreeable time

20. The pattern of an investigative interview is LARGELY set by the 20._____
    A. person being interviewed
    B. person conducting the interview
    C. nature of the investigation
    D. policy of the agency employing the interviewer

21. Assume that a person being interviewed, who had been talking freely, suddenly 21._____
    tries to change the subject.
    To a trained interviewer, this behavior would mean that the person PROBABLY
    A. knew very little about the subject
    B. realized that he was telling too much
    C. decided that his privacy was being violated
    D. realized that he was becoming confused

22. Assume that you, an investigator, receive a telephone call from an unknown 22._____
    individual requesting information about a case you are currently investigating.
    In such a situation, the BEST course of action for you to take is to
    A. give him the information over the telephone
    B. tell him to write to your department for the information
    C. send him the information, retaining a copy for your files
    D. tell him to call back, giving you additional time to check into the matter

23. Assume that you, an investigator, are responding to a written query from a 23._____
    member of the public protesting a certain procedure employed by your agency.
    In such a case, your response should stress MOST the
    A. difficulty that a large agency encounters in trying to treat all members of
       the public fairly
    B. idea that the procedure in question will be discontinued if enough
       complaints are received
    C. necessity for the procedure
    D. origin of the procedure

Questions 24-25.

DIRECTIONS: Questions 24 and 25 are to be answered in the light of the information given in
the following passage.

Assume that a certain agency is having a problem at one of its work locations because a sizable portion of the staff at that location is regularly tardy in reporting to work. The management of the agency is primarily concerned about eliminating the problem and is not yet too concerned about taking any disciplinary action. You are an investigator working for this agency, and though you have never had any contact with this location, you are assigned to investigate to determine, if possible, what might be causing this problem.

After several interviews, you see that low morale created by poor supervision at this location is at least part of the problem. Then, the last person you will interview before submitting your report tells you, when asked the reason for his tardiness, "*Well, I don't know; I just can't get up in the morning. So when I do get going, I've got to rush to get here. And just between you and me, I've lost interest in the job. Working conditions are bad, and it's hard for me to be enthusiastic about working here."*

24. Given the goals of the investigation and assuming that the investor was using a non-directive approach in this interview, of the following, the investigator's MOST effective response should be:
    A. *"You know, you are building a bad record of tardiness."*
    B. *"Can you tell me more about this situation?"*
    C. *"What kind of person is your superior?"*
    D. *"Do you think you are acting fairly towards the agency by being late so often?"*

    24._____

25. Given the goals of the investigation and assuming the investigator was using a directed approach in this interview, of the following, the investigator's response should be
    A. *"That doesn't seem like much of an excuse to me."*
    B. *"What do you mean by saying that you've lost interest?"*
    C. *What problems are there with the supervision you are getting?"*
    D. *"How do you think your tardiness looks in your personnel record?"*

    25._____

KEY (CORRECT ANSWERS)

1.	C		11.	D
2.	D		12.	B
3.	D		13.	B
4.	C		14.	C
5.	B		15.	C
6.	D		16.	A
7.	A		17.	D
8.	B		18.	D
9.	A		19.	C
10.	D		20.	B

21. B
22. B
23. C
24. B
25. C

EXAMINATION SECTION
TEST 1

DIRECTIONS: Each question or incomplete statement is followed by several suggested answers or completions. Select the one that BEST answers the question or completes the statement. *PRINT THE LETTER OF THE CORRECT ANSWER IN THE SPACE AT THE RIGHT.*

1. Which of the following is the BEST way to get an accurate account of an incident?
   A. Interview those involved immediately
   B. Interview those involved as soon as possibility
   C. Wait until you review the official reports and then interview those involved as soon as possible
   D. Carefully observe a videotaped simulation

2. While conducting investigations, it is necessary to pay close attention to nonverbal communication.
   This would include all of the following EXCEPT
   A. analyzing each individual's behavior as it arises
   B. paying attention to the person's tone of voice
   C. viewing the nonverbal messages as indicators
   D. noting discrepancies between verbal and nonverbal messages

3. While conducting an interview, it is MOST important to
   A. ignore your own values and past experiences
   B. utilize your own values and past experiences in recording information
   C. explain your own values to those you are interviewing
   D. be aware of your own values and experiences and of how they might influence the interview

4. Of the following, which is the BEST way to question a witness?
   A. Ask pointed questions   B. Talk in a clipped manner
   C. Talk aimlessly   D. Ask random questions

5. You are interviewing an uncooperative person.
   Of the following, the FIRST thing you should do in this situation is to
   A. try various appeal to win the person over to a cooperative attitude
   B. try to ascertain the reason for noncooperation
   C. promise the person that all data will be kept confidential
   D. alter the interviewing technique

6. Which of the following is the BEST way to make a witness feel at ease?
   A. Reassure him or her of the importance of the situation
   B. Tell the witness that any comments he or she makes will be of no use if the witness is too nervous

C. Allow the witness a little extra time to collect his or her thoughts
D. Maintain a friendly attitude

7. Which of the following behaviors would be the WORST to display during an investigative interview?
   A. Being unfocused
   B. Displaying uncertainty about some departmental regulations
   C. Acting biased
   D. Acting like you are overloaded with work

8. Investigations should be conducted with all of the following EXCEPT
   A. objectivity
   B. speed
   C. subjectivity
   D. thoroughness

9. When trying to help someone focus during an interview, it is BEST to
   A. use an open-ended question
   B. offer to reschedule at a time when the person is better prepared
   C. ask the person being interviewed to summarize the situation
   D. use a close-ended question

10. There are usually four stages during an interview: preparation, opening, conducting, and closing.
    All of the following are steps included in the closing stage of an interview EXCEPT
    A. verifying information
    B. stating the continuing responsibilities, if any, of the person being interviewed
    C. summarizing
    D. describing any additional steps that may need to be taken

11. During an employment interview, which of the following questions can legally be asked?
    A. What is your nationality?
    B. Are you at least 18 years of age?
    C. Do you wish to be addressed as Miss, Mrs. or Ms.?
    D. Do you have a disability?

12. As you continue talking with a man you are interviewing, you have the feeling that some of his answers to earlier questions were not totally correct. You think that he might have been afraid or confused earlier, but that the interview has now put him in a more comfortable frame of mind.
    In order to test the reliability of information received from the earlier questions, the BEST thing for you to do now is to ask new questions that
    A. allow him to explain why he deliberately gave you false information
    B. would yield the same information but are worded differently
    C. put pressure on him so that he personally wants to clear up the facts in his earlier answers
    D. indicate to him that you are aware of is deceptiveness

13. When investigating a situation, it is MOST important that those whom you have questioned
    A. feel that you are unbiased
    B. feel comfortable around you
    C. feel confident in your abilities
    D. admire your investigative skills

14. All of the following are examples of flight defenses EXCEPT
    A. rationalization
    B. talking about problems excessively
    C. using threatened language
    D. withdrawing

15. Assume that you have been assigned to conduct a follow-up interview with a primary witness whom you would like to have testify at an important hearing. Under these circumstances, it is MOST important to
    A. do your best to ensure that the witness remains cooperative
    B. conduct the matter in secret
    C. allow the witness to determine where and when the interview takes place
    D. conduct the interview as soon as possible to ensure a strong case

16. You are interviewing someone who is under a great deal of stress. He is talking continuously an rambling, making it difficult for you to obtain the information you need.
    In order to make the interview more successful, it would be BEST for you to
    A. interrupt him and ask him specific questions in order to get the information you need
    B. tell him that his rambling is causing you a lot of problems
    C. let him continue talking for as long as he wishes
    D. ask him to get to the point because you need to interview others

17. When an investigator first arrives at the scene of an incident, it is MOST important for him or her to be sure that
    A. all of the witnesses are telling the truth
    B. no additional physical evidence is destroyed
    C. all of the witnesses agree with each other about what they observed
    D. the witnesses do not become angry

18. All of the following statements about nonverbal communication are true EXCEPT:
    A. Nonverbal communication is easily controlled
    B. Much of the meaning of a message is transmitted through nonverbal behavior
    C. Nonverbal behaviors can reveal hidden agendas
    D. Nonverbal signals can help the interviewer determine if the person being interviewed is confused but unwilling to admit it

19. For state agencies, a properly conducted investigation might do any of the following EXCEPT
    A. discover the cause of a workplace accident
    B. uncover tax fraud or unfair labor practices by an employer

C. provide a supervisor with effective supervisory methods
D. uncover information critical to determining the outcome of an employee grievance

20. In interviewing, the practice of verbally anticipating the other person's answers to your questions is GENERALLY
    A. *desirable*, because it is effective and economical when interviewing large numbers of people
    B. *desirable*, because many people have language difficulties
    C. *undesirable*, because it is the right of every person to answer however he or she wishes
    D. *undesirable*, because the person being interviewed may be led to agree with the answer proposed by the interviewer even when the question is not entirely correct

KEY (CORRECT ANSWERS)

1.	A		11.	B
2.	A		12.	B
3.	D		13.	A
4.	A		14.	C
5.	B		15.	A
6.	D		16.	A
7.	C		17.	B
8.	C		18.	A
9.	D		19.	C
10.	A		20.	D

TEST 2

DIRECTIONS: Each question or incomplete statement is followed by several suggested answers or completions. Select the one that BEST answers the question or completes the statement. *PRINT THE LETTER OF THE CORRECT ANSWER IN THE SPACE AT THE RIGHT.*

1. All of the following are good examples of the volatile and vulnerable nature of evidence EXCEPT
    A. those involved may be intimidated to forget or to make up key elements of testimony
    B. physical evidence can disappear
    C. two extra copies are made of a valuable floppy disk
    D. water that caused an industrial accident can dry up

   1.____

2. You find that many of the people you interview are verbally abusive and unusually hostile to you.
   Of the following, the MOST appropriate action for you to take FIRST is to
    A. review your interviewing techniques and consider whether you may be somehow provoking those you interview
    B. act in a more authoritative manner when interviewing troublesome interviewees
    C. tell those people that you will not be able to help them unless their troublesome behavior ceases
    D. disregard the troublesome behavior and proceed as you would normally

   2.____

3. Of the following statements, which is the MOST accurate?
    A. Good investigative techniques are easily learned.
    B. Witnesses should be given a lot of time to collect their thoughts before being interviewed.
    C. The more standardized and thought-out the investigative procedures, the better the chance that the investigation will be successful.
    D. Statements taken from witnesses are not usually as critical to an investigation and subsequent action as some experts claim.

   3.____

4. The information sought in an interview is sometimes fixed in advance by a printed form or specific instructions from an interviewer's supervisor.
   Because of this, it is IMPORTANT to
    A. use your own judgment as to whether or not these questions should be used in the interview
    B. have the form in front of you so you can read from it and not miss any important points when interviewing
    C. make a copy of the form and give it to the client to complete
    D. be thoroughly acquainted with the purpose behind each question and understand its significance

   4.____

5. As an investigator, you perform field work in order to enforce state labor laws. If no set agency policy is in effect, it would MOST likely be the highest priority to investigate a report of

   5.____

A. a minimum wage violation
B. nonpayment of overtime wages to an employee
C. nonpayment to a worker in an industrial homework setting
D. systematic nonpayment to farm workers

6. In order to get the maximum amount of information from someone during an interview, it is MOST important for the interviewer to communicate to the person being interviewed the feeling that the interviewer is
    A. interested in what the person has to say
    B. a figure of authority
    C. efficient in his or her work habits
    D. sympathetic to the lifestyle of the person being interviewed

6._____

7. When an initial interview is being conducted, one way of starting is to explain the purpose of the interview to the person being interviewed.
The practice of starting the interview with such an explanation is GENERALLY
    A. *desirable*, because the person can then understand why the interview is necessary and what it should accomplish
    B. *desirable*, because it creates the rapport which is necessary to successful interviewing
    C. *undesirable*, because time will be saved if starting off directly with the questions which must be asked
    D. *undesirable*, because the interviewer should have the choice of starting an interview in the manner that he or she prefers

7._____

8. The GREATEST problem for investigators is when witnesses
    A. are so eager to cooperate that they frequently interrupt the investigator
    B. become a little bored telling and retelling what they have observed
    C. are not very willing to cooperate
    D. are eager to get back to work

8._____

9. Two important skills sometimes used during an interview are giving behavioral feedback and confronting.
What is the key difference between the two?
    A. There is none; they are actually two different names for the same process.
    B. Confronting is threatening, but giving behavioral feedback is not.
    C. Behavioral feedback merely describes action, while confronting evaluates the consequences of behavior.
    D. Behavioral feedback requires equipment in order to test the response of the client.

9._____

10. If applied properly, *being a good listener* is a desirable technique PRIMARILY because it
    A. more easily catches the person being interviewed in misrepresentations and lies
    B. conserves the energies of the interviewer

10._____

C. encourages the person being interviewed to talk about his or her personal affairs without restraint
D. is more likely to secure information which is generally reliable and complete

11. A full-scale police criminal investigation
    A. should be avoided at all costs
    B. may be warranted in some cases
    C. most likely means the agency investigator did not do his or her job properly
    D. is not necessary in state agencies

12. Which of the following are usually the MOST effective techniques for handling difficult behaviors during an interview?
    I. Focusing on nondefensive behaviors
    II. Respecting silence; letting yourself and the person you are interviewing get emotions under control
    III. Giving advice
    IV. Avoiding upsetting issues
    The CORRECT answer is:
    A. II, III   B. I, II   C. III, IV   D. I, III, IV

13. Assume that you are conducting safety and health inspections in a wide variety of settings. The supervisor at one of the sites you must periodically inspect seems very anxious during your visits and always wants you to pinpoint exactly when you will be returning for your next inspection.
    It would be BEST to
    A. assume the supervisor has something to hide, so you will double the number of inspections at the site
    B. assume nothing
    C. assume the supervisor is just slightly neurotic
    D. check to see if the supervisor has a criminal record

14. Of the following, the MOST important characteristic for an interviewer to have is
    A. personal attractiveness   B. sincerity
    C. appealing personality   D. a sense of humor

15. It is MOST likely that the longer the time before statements are taken from witnesses, the more
    A. time the witnesses will have to accurately reflect on what has occurred
    B. likely it is that the witnesses will be totally unwilling to cooperate
    C. likely it is that some distortion will occur
    D. likely it is that the witnesses will be willing to cooperate

16. The person you are interviewing is making, what you feel are, distasteful remarks. Of the following, the BEST approach would be to
    A. selectively ignore the remarks
    B. question the person about the remarks

C. confront the person
D. ask the person to stop or ask him or her to leave the interview

17. Which of the following behaviors should concern investigators the MOST? 17.____
    A. The tendency of eyewitnesses to *homogenize* what they have seen when exchanging information or chatting about the incident
    B. Eyewitnesses who are clear about minor details
    C. Eyewitnesses who are a little nervous
    D. Eyewitnesses who dislike their supervisors intensely

18. Part of your job requires the investigation of possible state sales tax fraud by organizations. 18.____
    Which of the following would MOST likely trigger a full-scale investigation?
    A. An anonymous phone call involving possible large-scale sales tax fraud by an organization
    B. A salesclerk forgets to add the sales tax to your order
    C. A new business does not have their sales tax *Certificate of Authority* prominently displayed so customers can see it
    D. The books and receipts of a large organization show that sales tax was not collected on $75 worth of merchandise

19. All of the following are inquiries that cannot be legally asked during an employment interview EXCEPT: 19.____
    A. Where were you born?
    B. Are you planning on having children?
    C. Are you able to carry out all necessary job assignments and perform them in a safe manner?
    D. In case of an emergency or accident, what is the name and address of the person to be notified?

20. When investigating a situation, you are careful when asking questions to never indicate how you think the question should be answered. 20.____
    This practice is a good idea PRIMARILY because
    A. it shows those you interview that you have confidence in their intelligence
    B. you will be more likely to get truthful answers
    C. you will not be significantly influencing the answers of those you have interviewed
    D. you will impress them with your interviewing skills

KEY (CORRECT ANSWERS)

1.	C	11.	B
2.	A	12.	B
3.	C	13.	B
4.	D	14.	B
5.	D	15.	C
6.	A	16.	A
7.	A	17.	A
8.	C	18.	A
9.	C	19.	C
10.	D	20.	C

EXAMINATION SECTION
TEST 1

DIRECTIONS: Each question or incomplete statement is followed by several suggested answers or completions. Select the one that BEST answers the question or completes the statement. *PRINT THE LETTER OF THE CORRECT ANSWER IN THE SPACE AT THE RIGHT.*

1. Assume that you are interviewing a witness who is telling a story crucial to your investigation. It is important that you get all the facts being related by this witness.
   In order to secure this vital information, the BEST of the following techniques is to
   A. quietly interrupt the witness's story and request him to speak with deliberation to that you can record his statement
   B. guide the witness during his recital so that all important points are validated
   C. confine your activities during the story to brief note-taking; and after the information has been secured, request a full written statement
   D. inform the witness that he must relate all the facts as truthfully and concisely as possible

2. The statement of any witness obtained by an investigator in an interview should GENERALLY be considered
   A. as a lead requiring substantiation by additional evidence
   B. accurate if the witness appears honest and is cooperative
   C. unreliable if the witness has been involved in similar investigations
   D. as a fact admissible under the rules of evidence

3. During an important interview, an investigator takes notes from time to time but very rarely looks at the subject being questioned.
   Such action on the part of the investigator is
   A. *unacceptable*, chiefly because during the actual interview an investigator should pay more attention to the witness's manner of giving the information rather than to the content of his statement
   B. *acceptable*, chiefly because data should be recorded at the earliest opportunity and important data should be noted meticulously
   C. *unacceptable*, chiefly because it inhibits the person being interviewed and is not conducive to a give-and-take discussion
   D. *acceptable*, chiefly because focusing attention on note-taking and not on the person being interviewed creates an impression of professional objectivity

4. The BEST source with which to check the credit rating of a business you are investigating is
   A. the Better Business Bureau
   B. Standard and Poor's
   C. Dun and Bradstreet, Inc.
   D. the State Attorney General's Office

5. Since he must, in the course of his investigations, interview persons with various personalities and attitudes, an investigator should GENERALLY adopt a method of interviewing that
   A. is uniformly applicable to all types so that discrepancies in the accounts of individuals may be readily detected
   B. can be adjusted to the persons whom he interviews
   C. is based on the premise that most witnesses tend to be uncooperative
   D. requires the investigator to spend as little time as possible in questioning witnesses

6. An investigator finds that X, Y, and Z are eyewitnesses to an incident under investigation. He interviews X, who gives him a complete and very detailed statement about the incident. X also informs the investigator that he has discussed the matter with Y and Z, and that each of them completely agrees with him as to what had occurred.
   Under these circumstances, it would be MOST appropriate for the investigator to
   A. interview Y and Z before assessing the value of the statements made by the three witnesses
   B. interview Y and Z and accept their versions if they both disagree with the story given by witness X
   C. interview either Y or Z and close the investigation if the statement of either witness agrees with the story given by witness X
   D. close the investigation on the basis of his interview with witness X since there is no reason to assume that Y and Z will tell a different story

7. Which one of the following is a legal requirement for the admissibility of evidence in a legal procedure?
   A. Weight   B. Sufficiency   C. Competency   D. Recency

8. Of the following diagrams, which one represents the CORRECT utilization of the ABC Method of Surveillance?
   Note: S identifies the suspect's position
   X identifies the positions of investigators
   Arrow indicates direction in which suspect is moving

3 (#1)

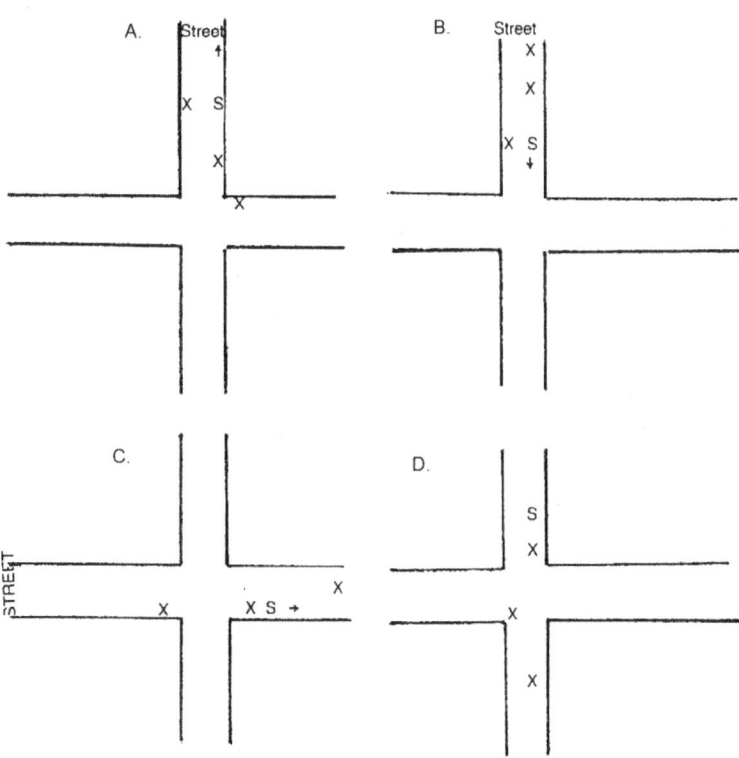

9. During an interview, an interviewee makes the following statement: *I have given the problem of getting a job a great deal of thought. I am looking primarily for an opportunity to grow and develop—to find the type of job that will provide the greatest challenge and bring out the best that is in me. Security probably ranks at the bottom of my list since I feel that I can always make a living somewhere.*
From an analysis of this statement, an investigator would be LEAST likely to conclude that the interviewee is
   A. capable of analytical thought
   B. looking for job satisfaction
   C. seeking self-improvement
   D. trying to cover for his lack of self-confidence

9._____

10. One of the more difficult tasks facing an investigator in an interview is to control the tendency of witnesses to ramble when giving information.
Of the following, the BEST technique for keeping a witness's comments pertinent is to
   A. ask questions which indicate the desired answer
   B. insist on *yes* and *no* answers to his questions
   C. construct questions that restrict the range of information which the witness can give in response
   D. ask precise questions so that the answers of the witness will necessarily be brief

10._____

4 (#1)

11. The BASIC purpose of producing evidence in legal proceedings is to
    A. provide a permanent official record for legal action
    B. screen out confusing issues of law and fact
    C. determine the truth of a matter in issue
    D. insure that hearsay statements will be excluded

12. An investigator is handling a case involving an individual and find that the case is proving very difficult because he has run out of leads to follow up.
    Of the following, the BEST way for the investigator to deal with this case is FIRST to
    A. prepare a report of the case indicating that no further action can be taken
    B. place himself in the position of the person being investigated
    C. re-interview all those affected by the case until a new clue is revealed
    D. wait for the first break in the case which will give a substantial lead

13. Assume that you need to interview a person who is suspected of collaborating with the subject under investigation.
    Of the following, the interviewing procedure that is MOST appropriate for handling this situation is to
    A. conduct a casual interview with the person on a pretext different from the actual purpose of the interview
    B. interview the person intensively by means of the *team* method until he breaks down and gives information
    C. insist that the suspected person cooperate
    D. plan to review every statement made by the person until he realizes that no fact will be overlooked

14. Assume that two disinterested individuals had directly witnessed the same event. An investigator who interviewed them received two distinctly different versions of this event.
    Which of the following assumptions PROBABLY accounts for the difference in the two versions?
    A. The event must have consisted of so many separate happenings that no one could understand everything that occurred.
    B. Each individual was selective in his perception of the event.
    C. The interviewing technique used by the investigator was instrumental in eliciting different facts from each individual.
    D. One of the individuals wishes to cooperate with the investigator, but the other did not.

15. During interviews, a certain investigator phrases follow-up questions mentally during pauses while the subject is still answering the previous question.
    This practice is GENERALLY
    A. *desirable*, chiefly because it gives the impression that the investigator is well-acquainted with all the facts
    B. *undesirable*, chiefly because the investigator cannot know whether such questions will be appropriate

C. *desirable*, chiefly because it enables the investigator to pose new questions without significant breaks in the discussion
D. *undesirable*, chiefly because it subjects the person being interviewed to a barrage of questions

16. Generally, a professional investigator's practice of training himself to give the impression of telling the truth during court appearances is considered
    A. *desirable*, chiefly because only by such practice can he perfect his ability to give accurate testimony
    B. *undesirable*, chiefly because any deviation from the unadulterated truth by using a pretension constitutes perjury
    C. *desirable*, chiefly because such training lessens the possibility of his appearing nervous and timid while testifying, which might convey the impression that he is evasive or lying
    D. *undesirable*, chiefly because all testimony should be given in a natural manner, including hesitations, to avoid the court's suspicion that the witness has been coached

17. Assume that prior to an interview, a person makes a spontaneous declaration relating to his case in the presence of an investigator.
    According to a rule of evidence, the person's statement is GENERALLY
    A. *admissible*, only if the investigator testifies to the declaration and his testimony is corroborated by another person
    B. *inadmissible*, chiefly because it constitutes a hearsay declaration against the person's interest
    C. *admissible*, chiefly because it was not the product of the person's deliberation and reflection
    D. *inadmissible*, chiefly because the person was under duress when the exclamation was made

18. In order to break down the communication barriers between an interviewer and his subject, the interviewer should GENERALLY ask introductory questions which
    A. focus on the individual's job status
    B. can be answered in a *yes-or-no* fashion
    C. focus directly on official business
    D. are likely to be of mutual interest to the two parties

19. To introduce as evidence a set of business books prepared by a person other than the individual under investigation, preliminary evidence pertaining to the content of the books must first be established.
    Which of the following does NOT constitute a fact which must be established before such books may be admitted as evidence?
    A. entries were made in the regular course of business at or about the time of the transactions involved
    B. books have been audited and certified as correct
    C. books are the regular books used for making business entries
    D. entries in the books were made by persons required to make them in the course of their regular duties

20. A person who is suffering from a mental disability is not necessarily disqualified from testifying as a witness in a legal proceeding PROVIDED that such person
    A. has the ability to recall and describe past events pertaining to the case
    B. is not an inmate of a mental institution
    C. is attended by a qualified psychiatrist at all times while in the courtroom
    D. swears that he knows the difference between right and wrong

20.____

21. Of the following public records, which is the BEST single source of information on the personal history and background of a subject?
    A. Birth or baptismal certificate
    B. Marriage license application
    C. Discharge certificate from the military services
    D. Income tax return

21.____

22. When it is necessary to prove the contents of a written instrument concerning a matter in dispute, the *best evidence rule* provides that
    A. the contents of written instruments must be subscribed and sworn to before a notary public to be admissible in legal proceedings
    B. no evidence outside the instrument itself shall be used to alter the wording of the instrument
    C. a witness who qualifies as an expert in handwriting identification shall first testify on the genuineness of the instrument
    D. the original instrument itself must be produced in court if it is available

22.____

23. Public documents, if otherwise competent, are admissible as evidence of the facts recorded therein, without the testimony of the officers who entered the facts, CHIEFLY because
    A. public records are subject to such strict security that the entries therein cannot be altered or falsified
    B. all such documents require further corroboration before they are admissible as proof of any facts recorded therein
    C. entries in these documents are made by officers who have sworn to perform their duties in the public interest
    D. hearsay evidence may not be admitted to prove a fact in dispute without the testimony of the officer who recorded it

23.____

24. One of the following ways in which an investigator might ordinarily detect an inconsistency in an interviewee's story is by
    A. having a third party present during the interview
    B. requesting the subject to speak more slowly
    C. observing the subject's manner of dress or attire
    D. watching the subject's facial expressions and mannerisms

24.____

25. The use of small talk or conversation about extraneous topics such as sports, the weather, or current events at the start of a routine interview designed to elicit information is GENERALLY considered
    A. *desirable*, chiefly because it gives the subject a chance to relax and relieve himself of the tension that normally develops before an interview

25.____

B. *undesirable*, chiefly because it wastes the valuable time of subjects with matters that are unrelated to the purpose of the interview
C. *desirable*, chiefly because it is the only way the interviewer is able to ascertain whether he and the subject will be able to develop rapport
D. *undesirable*, chiefly because it is possible to obtain more information about the subject if he is unaware of the purpose of the interview

26. Assume that your superior assigns you to interview an individual who, he warns, seems to be highly *introverted*.
You should be aware that, during an interview, such a person is likely to
A. hold views which are highly controversial in nature
B. be domineering and try to control the direction of the interview
C. resist answering personal questions regarded his background
D. give information which is largely fabricated

27. The one of the following persons who is MOST likely to be willing to give information leading to the apprehension of a suspect is someone who is
A. friendly with the suspect
B. afraid of the subject
C. interested in law enforcement
D. seeking revenge against the suspect

28. During the course of a routine interview, the BEST tone of voice for an interviewer to use is
A. authoritative   B. uncertain   C. formal   D. conversational

29. It is recommended that interviews which inquire into the personal background of an individual should be held in private.
The BEST reason for this practice is that privacy
A. allows the individual to talk freely about the details of his background
B. induces contemplative thought on the part of the interviewed individual
C. prevents any interruptions by departmental personnel during the interview
D. most closely resembles the atmosphere of the individual's personal life

30. Of the following, the MOST preferable way for an investigator to make a reference check on a subject's previous employment in the area is to
A. write to the employer and ask him to fill out a standard employee evaluation form
B. call the employer and conduct a telephone interview
C. write to the employer and request a personal interview
D. telephone the employer and ask him to submit a written evaluation

31. Of the following, the BEST way for an investigator to prepare himself for a court appearance as a witness is generally by
A. memorizing every detail of the case in order to give an exact recital of the information
B. reviewing his notes and trying to fix in his mind the highlights of the case

C. consulting with his superiors in order to ascertain which aspects of the case should be emphasized
D. studying all aspects of the case and writing out in detail the testimony he intends to give under oath

32. When an investigator is called as a witness to relate a series of incidents, his testimony should GENERALLY consist of
    A. a background narrative, followed by important facts and a concluding statement
    B. important facts, followed by a background narrative and a concluding statement
    C. details personally observed followed by any undeveloped leads
    D. a simple chronological account of the events he has observed

33. Of the following, an individual who smokes heavily during interrogation or an interview is LEAST likely to experience a(n)
    A. decrease in mental efficiency
    B. decrease in physical efficiency
    C. state of high emotion during questioning
    D. emotional release during questioning

34. The BEST way for an investigator to handle a situation in which the person interviewed asks a few slightly personal questions is generally to
    A. give quick, evasive answers and continue with the interview
    B. tell the person such questions are irrelevant and objectionable
    C. inquire fully into the person's reasons for wanting such information
    D. answer the questions briefly and truthfully

35. The CHIEF purpose of using surveillance in an investigation is to
    A. obtain information about persons and activities
    B. cause suspected persons to feel continuously uneasy
    C. maintain a close watch over hostile witnesses
    D. induce subjects to volunteer information

36. A *surreptitious* recording of an interview is one which is made
    A. whenever the information is highly technical
    B. to conceal the identity of the interviewee
    C. without the knowledge of the subject
    D. to encourage a subject to be more informative

37. All the means by which any alleged matter of fact, the truth of which is submitted to investigation, is established or disproved is the legal definition of
    A. proof   B. burden of proof
    C. evidence   D. admissibility of evidence

38. That section of an affidavit in which an officer empowered to administer an oath certifies that this document was sworn to before him is called a(n)
    A. affirmation   B. jurat
    C. acknowledgement D. verification

39. In legal terminology, a *bailee* is a person who
    A. lawfully holds property belonging to another
    B. deposits cash or property for the release of an arrested person
    C. has been released from arrest on a bond that guarantees his court appearance
    D. deposits personal property as collateral for a debt

40. A specimen of handwriting of known authorship which can be used by an investigator for making a comparison with a questioned or suspected writing is called a(n)
    A. inscription   B. precis   C. coordinate   D. exemplar

41. The attorney felt that his client would be *exonerated*.
    In this sentence, *exonerated* means MOST NEARLY
    A. unwilling to testify
    B. declared blameless
    C. severely punished
    D. placed on probation

42. The two witnesses were suspected of *collusion*.
    In this sentence, the word *collusion* means MOST NEARLY
    A. a conflict of interest
    B. an unintentional error
    C. an illegal secret agreement
    D. financial irregularities

43. Many of the subject's answers during the interview were *redundant*.
    In this sentence, *redundant* means MOST NEARLY
    A. uninformative   B. thoughtful   C. repetitious   D. argumentative

44. He was assigned to investigate an individual who was *insolvent*.
    In this sentence, *insolvent* means MOST NEARLY
    A. unable to pay debts
    B. extremely disrespectful
    C. difficult to understand
    D. frequently out of work

45. In his report, the investigator described several *covert* business transactions.
    In this sentence, *covert* means MOST NEARLY
    A. unauthorized   B. joint   C. complicated   D. secret

KEY (CORRECT ANSWERS)

1. C	11. C	21. B	31. B	41. B
2. A	12. B	22. D	32. D	42. C
3. C	13. A	23. C	33. C	43. C
4. C	14. B	24. D	34. D	44. A
5. B	15. C	25. A	35. A	45. D
6. A	16. C	26. C	36. C	
7. C	17. C	27. D	37. C	
8. C	18. D	28. D	38. B	
9. D	19. B	29. A	39. A	
10. C	20. A	30. A	40. D	

TEST 2

DIRECTIONS: Each question or incomplete statement is followed by several suggested answers or completions. Select the one that BEST answers the question or completes the statement. *PRINT THE LETTER OF THE CORRECT ANSWER IN THE SPACE AT THE RIGHT.*

Questions 1-5.

DIRECTIONS: Questions 1 through 5 consist of two sentences which may or may not contain errors in word usage or sentence structure, punctuation, or capitalization. Consider a sentence correct although there may be other correct ways of expressing the same thought.
Mark your answer:
A. If only Sentence I is correct;
B. If only sentence II is correct;
C. If Sentences I and II are both correct;
D. If Sentences I and II are both incorrect.

1. I. Being locked in his desk, the investigator felt sure that the records would be safe.
    II. The reason why the witness changed his statement was because he had been threatened.

2. I. The investigation had just began then an important witness disappeared.
    II. The check that had been missing was located and returned to its owner, Harry Morgan, a resident of Suffolk County, New York.

3. I. A supervisor will find that the establishment of standard procedures enables his staff to work more efficiently.
    II. An investigator hadn't ought to give any recommendations in his report if he is in doubt.

4. I. Neither the investigator nor his supervisor is ready to interview the witnesses.
    II. Interviewing has been and always will be an important asset in investigation.

5. I. One of the investigator's reports has been forwarded to the wrong person.
    II. The investigator stated that he was not familiar with those kind of cases.

Questions 6-8.

DIRECTIONS: Questions 6 through 8 are to be answered SOLELY on the basis of the following passage.

As investigators, we are more concerned with the utilitarian than the philosophical aspects of ethics and ethical standards, procedures, and conduct. As a working consideration, we might view ethics as the science of doing the right thing at the right time in the right manner in conformity with the normal, everyday standards imposed by society; and in conformity with the judgment society would be expected to make concerning the rightness or wrongness of what we have done.

An ethical code might be considered a basic set of rules and regulations to which we must conform in the performance of investigative duties. Ethical standards, procedures, and conduct might be considered the logical workings of our ethical code in its everyday application to our work. Ethics also necessarily involves morals and morality. We must eventually answer the self-imposed question of whether or not we have acted in the right way in conducting our investigative activities in their individual and total aspects.

6. Of the following, the MOST suitable title for the above passage is 6.____
   A. The Importance of Rules for Investigators
   B. The Basic Philosophy of a Lawful Society
   C. Scientific Aspects of Investigations
   D. Ethical Guidelines For the Conduct of Investigations

7. According to the above passage, ethical considerations for investigators involve 7.____
   A. special standards that are different from those which apply to the rest of society
   B. practices and procedures which cannot be evaluated by others
   C. individual judgments by investigators of the appropriateness of their own actions
   D. regulations which are based primarily upon a philosophical approach

8. Of the following, the author's PRINCIPAL purpose in writing the above passage seems to have been to 8.____
   A. emphasize the importance of self-criticism in investigative activities
   B. explain the relationship that exists between ethics and investigative conduct
   C. reduce the amount of unethical conduct in the area of investigations
   D. seek recognition by his fellow investigators for his academic treatment of the subject matter

Questions 9-11.

DIRECTIONS: Questions 9 through 11 are to be answered SOLELY on the basis of the following passage.

The investigator must remember that acts of omission can be as effective as acts of commission in affecting the determination of disputed issues. Acts of omission, such as failure to obtain available information or failure to verify dubious information, manifest themselves in miscarriages of justice and erroneous adjudications. An incomplete investigation is an erroneous investigation because a conclusion predicated upon inadequate facts is based on quicksand.

When an investigator throws up his hands and admits defeat, the reason for this action does not necessarily lie in his possible laziness and ineptitude. It is more likely that the investigator has made his conclusions after exhausting only those avenues of investigation of which he is aware. He has exercised good faith in his belief that nothing else can be done.

This tendency must be overcome by all investigators if they are to operate at top efficiency. If no suggestion for new or additional action can be found in any authority, an investigator should use his own initiative to cope with a given situation. No investigator should ever hesitate to set precedents. It is far better in the final analysis to attempt difficult solutions, even if the chances of error are obviously present, than it is to take refuge in the spinless adage: If you don't do anything, you don't do it wrong.

9. Of the following, the MOST suitable title for the above passage is
   A. The Need For resourcefulness in Investigations
   B. Procedures For Completing an Investigation
   C. The Development of Standards For Investigators
   D. The Causes of Incomplete Investigations

10. Of the following, the author of this passage considers that the LEAST important consideration in developing new investigative methods is
    A. efficiency
    B. caution
    C. imagination
    D. thoroughness

11. According to this passage, which of the following statements is INCORRECT?
    A. Lack of creativity may lead to erroneous investigations.
    B. Acts of omission are sometimes as harmful as acts of commission.
    C. Some investigators who give up on a case are lazy or inept.
    D. An investigator who gives up on a case is usually not acting in good faith.

Questions 12-15.

DIRECTIONS: Questions 12 through 15 are to be answered SOLELY on the basis of the following passage.

Perpetrators of crimes are often described by witnesses or victims in terms of salient facial features. The Bertillon System of Identification, which preceded the widespread use of fingerprints, was based on body measurements. Recently, there have been developments in the quantification of procedures used in the classification and comparison of facial characteristics. Devices are now available which enable a trained operator, with the aid of a witness, to form a composite picture of a suspect's face and to translate that composite into a numerical code. Further developments in this area are possible, using computers to develop efficient sequences of questions so that witnesses may quickly arrive at the proper description.

Recent studies of voice analysis and synthesis, originally motivated by problems of efficient telephone transmission, have led to the development of the audio-frequency profile or "voice print." Each voice print may be sufficiently unique to permit development of a classification system that will make possible positive identification of the source of a voice print. This method of identification, using an expert to identify the voice patterns, has been introduced in more than 40 cases by 15 different police departments. As with all identification systems that rely on experts to perform the identification, controlled laboratory tests are needed to establish with care the relative frequency of errors of omission and commission made by experts.

12. The MOST appropriate title for the above passage is   12.____
    A. Technology in Modern Investigative Detection
    B. Identification By Physical Features
    C. Verification of Identifications By Experts
    D. The Use of Electronic Identification Techniques

13. According to the above passage, computers may be used in conjunction with   13.____
    which of the following identification techniques?
    A. Fingerprints   B. Bertillon System
    C. Voice prints   D. Composite facial pictures

14. According to the above passage, the ability to identify individuals based on   14.____
    facial characteristics has improved as a result of
    A. an increase in the number of facial types which can be shown to witnesses
    B. information which is derived from other body measurements
    C. coded classification and comparison techniques
    D. greater reliance upon experts to make the identifications

15. According to the above passage, it is CORRECT to state that audio-frequency   15.____
    profiles or voice prints
    A. have been decisive in many prosecutions
    B. reduce the number of errors made by experts
    C. developed as a result of problems in telephonic communications
    D. are unlikely to result in positive identifications

Questions 16-20.

DIRECTIONS: Questions 16 through 20 are to be answered SOLELY on the basis of the following graph.

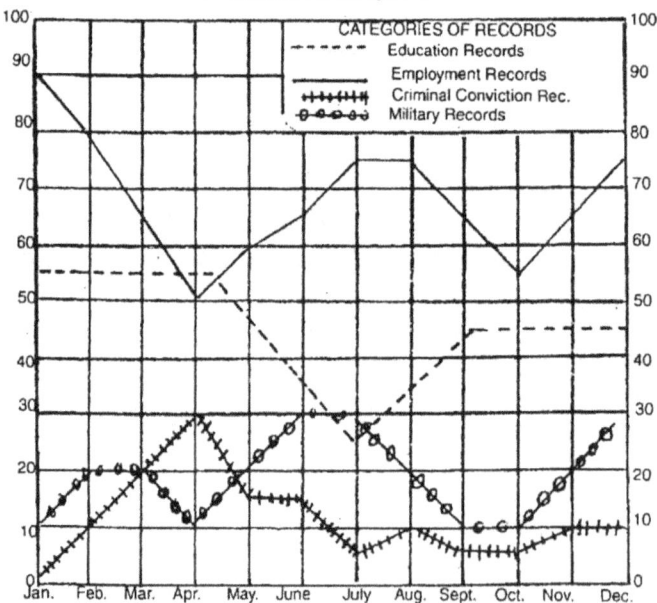

EMPLOYMENT APPLICATION INFORMATION
CHECKED BY INVESTIGATORS IN DEPARTMENT Z
CENTRAL CITY

16. The category for which the SMALLEST number of record checks was made in _____ records.
    A. education
    B. employment
    C. criminal conviction
    D. military

    16._____

17. In which of the following months did the combined number of criminal conviction record checks and military record checks EXCEED the number of education record checks?
    A. March
    B. April
    C. May
    D. June

    17._____

18. During which of the following months was the total number of records checked LARGEST?
    A. March
    B. April
    C. September
    D. November

    18._____

19. Which of the following statements is INCORRECT according to the graph?
    A. Employment records checked each month always exceeded 45.
    B. Education records checked in February did not equal the number of education records checked in November.
    C. Military records checked per month increased from October to December.
    D. Criminal conviction records checked in any given month never exceeded the number of military records checked.

    19._____

20. Of the total number of records checked in March, the percentage that were education records was MOST NEARLY
    A. 13%
    B. 25%
    C. 34%
    D. 41%

    20._____

Questions 21-25.

DIRECTIONS: Questions 21 through 25 are to be answered SOLELY on the basis of the information contained in the following tables.

STATUS OF TAX CASES ASSIGNED TO INVESTIGATORS, FISCAL YEAR, CENTRAL CIT, DEPARTMENT Y

Investigator	Cases Assigned	Cases Completed	Cases Pending at End of Fiscal Year
Albert	70	50	20
Bennett	90	60	30
Gordon	82	50	32
Nolton	70	40	30
Paxton	75	50	25
Rich	80	60	20

STATUS OF MISCELLANEOUS CASES ASSIGNED TO INVESTIGATORS
FISCAL YEAR, CENTRAL CITY, DEPARTMENT Y

Investigator	Cases Assigned	Cases Completed	Cases Pending at End of Fiscal Year
Albert	25	20	5
Bennett	20	15	5
Gordon	18	13	5
Nolton	30	23	7
Paxton	17	17	0
Rich	32	24	6

21. Of the following, the investigator who completed the GREATEST percentage of his assigned tax cases in the fiscal year was
    A. Albert   B. Gordon   C. Paxton   D. Rich

22. The total number of the tax cases assigned in the fiscal year EXCEEDED the total number of miscellaneous cases assigned by
    A. 142   B. 325   C. 400   D. 467

23. Of the following, the two investigators who completed the SAME percentage of the miscellaneous cases assigned to them were
    A. Albert and Gordon
    B. Gordon and Nolton
    C. Nolton and Paxton
    D. Bennett and Rich

24. The average number of cases (both tax and miscellaneous) pending per investigator at the end of the fiscal year was MOST NEARLY
    A. 31   B. 28   C. 26   D. 5

25. Assume that the total number of miscellaneous cases pending at the end of the fiscal year is equal to 25% of the number of cases pending at the end of the previous fiscal year.
    What was the TOTAL number of miscellaneous cases pending at the end of the previous fiscal year?
    A. 28   B. 56   C. 74   D. 112

26. The head of an agency, in addressing a group of investigators, stated, *Whenever possible, do all you can to satisfy the needs of members of the public.*
    Which of the following is the LEAST acceptable procedure for investigators to use in implementing this policy?
    A. Handle public grievances and frustrations before they can accumulate.
    B. Satisfy public demands even though organizational goals may be compromised.
    C. Interpret rules and regulations reasonably.
    D. Use mass media to enlist support of programs to win public cooperation.

7 (#2)

27. Of the following, the MOST important purpose of having a citizen advisory committee in a public agency is to
    A. make both the citizen groups and the public agency more responsive to the total public interest
    B. prevent fraud and mismanagement within the administration of the agency
    C. improve efficiency and encourage greater diligence on the part of agency personnel
    D. prevent the spread of unfavorable publicity about the agency's activities

27.____

28. Of the following, the term *public relations* in its application to any public agency is BEST defined as
    A. all the publicity received by the agency
    B. all the direct and indirect contacts between the agency itself and the clientele it deals with
    C. the sum total of efforts which the agency directs toward performing its functions
    D. de-emphasis of the agency's basic obligations which are not popular with its clientele

28.____

29. Assume that you receive a phone call from a man who refuses to identify himself and insists that he *knows for a fact* that an investigator on the staff of your agency has destroyed incriminating records upon receipt of a bribe.
The MOST appropriate action for you to take would be to
    A. refuse to discuss the matter unless the caller gives you his name and additional identification
    B. ask the caller for the facts and the name of the suspected investigator
    C. advise the caller that such a serious charge should be reported immediately to the police department
    D. politely advise the caller to report the facts in a letter to your agency head

29.____

30. In a public agency, the FIRST step in adopting a system which will give citizens an opportunity to make complaints against the agency's staff members is to
    A. establish an adequate complaint procedure
    B. design a citizen complaint report form
    C. establish physical facilities where complaints to the agency may be received
    D. initiate a public relations campaign informing the public that they may file complaints

30.____

31. Which of the following kinds of information is NOT found in the Official Directory of the City (Green Book)?
    A. The number of persons employed in each city agency
    B. A listing of police station houses and fire engine companies in each borough
    C. The names and addresses of all public high schools and city hospitals in each borough
    D. The names and addresses of federal, state, and city courts located within the city

31.____

32. An investigator should contact the State Department of Health to obtain information about persons who are licensed or qualified to practice as
    A. x-ray technicians
    B. physiotherapists
    C. chiropractors
    D. pharmacists

33. An employee complains that the city has refused to pay him some back salary for services he performed last year.
    This employee may bring legal action in the Small Claims Part if the amount of his claim does NOT exceed
    A. $1,000   B. $1,500   C. $300   D. $100

34. Experienced investigators have found that using the question-and-answer method in interviewing a witness, instead of allowing the witness to tell his own story freely and without interruption, MOST often tends to _____ the accuracy of the information given by the witness.
    A. *increase* both the scope and
    B. *increase* the scope but *decrease*
    C. *decrease* both the scope and
    D. *decrease* the scope but *increase*

35. Of the following, the STRONGEST indication that the signature on an important document is a forgery is that the suspected signature
    A. is partly illegible
    B. shows a noticeable trembling in certain letters
    C. shows that the writer retouched several letters
    D. is identical in all respects with a signature known to be genuine

36. Prior to writing the complete and final report at the conclusion of an important case, some investigators prepare an outline or blueprint of the investigative data compiled.
    All of the following are important advantages of preparing such an outline or blueprint EXCEPT that it
    A. results in the omission of less important or minor facts
    B. helps in achieving logical arrangement of the materials
    C. lessens chances of omitting essential details
    D. aids in recognizing irrelevant details

37. In determining the validity of a document, the use of oblique lighting renders certain kinds of alterations visible.
    Which of the following alterations would NOT be exposed by use of the oblique lighting technique?
    A. Abrasions and erasures made in order to change some significant part of a document
    B. Rubber-stamp impressions intended to violate a document but made from a non-genuine stamp
    C. Tears, mutilations, or excessive foldings made deliberately in order to conceal or obscure some damaging feature of the document
    D. Traced writing or writing taken from some pattern or model of genuine writing

38. When an investigator takes the witness stand for the prosecution, he must realize that the opposing counsel will GENERALLY endeavor to portray him as a(n)
    A. individual whose moral character is questionable and whose veracity therefore should be doubted
    B. disinterested collector and retailer of facts
    C. interested party who is trying to convict his client on the basis of insufficient evidence
    D. unprejudiced official with competent professional experience

38.____

39. Assume that on a certain day, an investigator finds that he has an excessive number of appointments for interviews and believes that he will be unable to keep them all during the course of the day.
Of the following, the BEST action he could take is to
    A. ask a fellow investigator to help him conduct a group interview
    B. interview the maximum number that can be interviewed properly and reschedule the others for a future date
    C. proceed according to the established schedule
    D. shorten the length of time spent interviewing each person in order to insure that everyone is interviewed

39.____

40. There has been a tendency in recent times to publicize the use of instrumentation such as lie detectors, electronic eavesdropping devices, special cameras, and other technical devices in civil and criminal investigations.
Of the following statements, the one which expresses a MAJOR weakness which results from relying too much on instrumentation as an investigative aid is:
    A. The use of these technical devices invariably violates the constitutional rights of persons subject to investigations
    B. Excessive publicity in the mass media about the success of these mechanical devices in solving difficult cases destroys their value as investigative aids
    C. These technical devices have a very limited value in cases where abundant physical evidence is available
    D. Inexperienced investigators are prone to place their faith in technical methods to the neglect of the more basic investigative procedures

40.____

KEY (CORRECT ANSWERS)

1.	D	11.	D	21.	D	31.	A
2.	B	12.	B	22.	B	32.	A
3.	A	13.	D	23.	D	33.	B
4.	C	14.	C	24.	A	34.	B
5.	A	15.	C	25.	D	35.	D
6.	D	16.	C	26.	B	36.	A
7.	C	17.	D	27.	A	37.	B
8.	B	18.	A	28.	B	38.	C
9.	A	19.	D	29.	B	39.	B
10.	B	20.	C	30.	A	40.	D

EXAMINATION SECTION
TEST 1

DIRECTIONS: Each question or incomplete statement is followed by several suggested answers or completions. Select the one that BEST answers the question or completes the statement. *PRINT THE LETTER OF THE CORRECT ANSWER IN THE SPACE AT THE RIGHT.*

1. If S, the subject that investigator H is tailing, enters a large department store, H should
    A. wait outside the store in a concealed place until S comes out
    B. follow S into the store
    C. enter the store, but wait by the door
    D. wait outside the store but in a position near the door S entered

    1._____

2. Which of the following is MOST likely to indicate an attempt at falsification of a particular document?
    A. Change in style of handwriting within the document
    B. Illegible writing
    C. Erasures or alterations
    D. Folds or creases in the document

    2._____

3. A subject being tailed during a foot surveillance quickly turns and confronts the shadower and states, *Say, Bud, are you tailing me?*
    Of the following, the MOST appropriate action for the shadower to take is to
    A. ignore the question and keep on walking
    B. admit that he is shadowing the subject but refuse to tell him why
    C. deny the accusation but give no explanations
    D. give some excuse for his presence in the form of a cover-up

    3._____

4. K, an investigator, has been given the assignment of tailing S, a suspect, who will be traveling by car at night in the city.
    Of the following, the SIMPLEST way for K to carry out this surveillance would be to
    A. mark S's car beforehand so it is identifiable at night
    B. memorize the model, color, and style of S's car
    C. memorize the license plate of S's car
    D. mechanically disable S's car so it will be unusable

    4._____

5. The United States Treasury Department may prove to be a valuable source of information in specialized instances.
    Which of the following types of information usually would NOT be in the custody of that Federal agency?
    A. Immigration records
    B. Records of licensed manufacturers of narcotics
    C. Importers and exporters records
    D. Records of persons or firms manufacturing alcohol

    5._____

6. Which of the following is a writ directing that documents or records be produced in court?
   A. Writ of habeas corpus
   B. Subpoena habeas corpus
   C. Order, pro hoc vice
   D. Subpoena duces tecum

7. *Modus Operandi* is a phrase frequently used in investigative work to refer to a
   A. specific type of investigation
   B. particular policy in tracing missing persons
   C. manner in which a criminal operates
   D. series of crimes committed by more than one person

8. P, an investigator, has been assigned to interview W, a witness, concerning a minor automobile accident. Although P has made no breach of the basic rules of contact and approach, he nevertheless recognizes that he and W have a personality clash and that a natural animosity has resulted.
   Of the following, P MOST appropriately should
   A. discuss the personality problem with W and attempt to resolve the difference
   B. stop the interview on some pretext and leave in a calm and pleasant manner, allowing an associate to continue the interview
   C. ignore the personality problem and continue as though nothing had happened
   D. change the subject matter being discussed since the facts sought may be the source of the animosity

9. Assume that an investigator desires to interview W, a reluctant witness to a bribery attempt that took place several weeks previously. Assume further that the interview can take place at a location to be designated by the interviewer.
   Of the following, the place of interview should PREFERABLY be the
   A. office of the interviewer
   B. home of W
   C. office of W
   D. scene where the event took place

10. Assume that T, an investigator, is testifying in court. He does not clearly remember the details of the incident about which he is testifying.
    Of the following, the MOST appropriate action for T to take is to
    A. admit he does not remember the details and go on to the next question
    B. look at his statement previously given to the attorney interviewing him before trial
    C. refresh his memory by referring to his notebook
    D. testify to only those items he can recall

11. Assume that as an investigator you are interviewing W, a witness. During the interview, it becomes apparent that W's statements are inaccurate and at variance with the facts previously established.
    In these circumstances, it would be BEST for you to
    A. tell W that his statements are inaccurate and point out how they conflict with previously established facts

B. reword your questions and ask additional questions about the facts being discussed
C. warn W that he may be required to testify under oath at a later date
D. ignore W's statements if you have other information that support the facts

12. Assume that W, a witness being interviewed by you, an investigator, shows a tendency to ramble. His answers to your questions are lengthy and not responsive.
In this situation, the BEST action for you to take is to
    A. permit W to continue because at some point he will tell you the information sought
    B. tell W that he is rambling and unresponsive and that more will be accomplished if he is brief and to the point
    C. control the interview so that complete and accurate information is obtained
    D. patiently listen to W since rambling is W's style and it cannot be changed

13. Assume that an investigator is to interview a witness.
Of the following, the BEST procedure for the investigator to follow in regard to the use of his notebook is to
    A. take out his notebook at the start of the interview and immediately begin taking notes
    B. memorize the important facts related during the interview and enter them after the interview has been completed
    C. advise the witness that all his answers are being taken down to insure that he will tell the truth
    D. establish rapport with the witness and ask permission to jot down various data in his notebook

14. The first duty of the investigator who has in his possession a document which may be used in evidence is to preserve it in its original condition.
Following are three actions which might constitute rules for the handling of a document:
I. Pick up the document with tweezers or a pin
II. Staple the document to a folder so that it is protected
III. Photograph or photocopy the document
Which one of the following choices MOST accurately classifies the above statements into those which are APPROPRIATE and those which are NOT APPROPRIATE as procedures for handling such documents?
    A. I and III are appropriate, but II is not appropriate
    B. I and II are appropriate, but III is not appropriate
    C. II is appropriate, but I and III are not appropriate
    D. III is appropriate, but I and II are not appropriate

15. Of the following, which one would be the CLEAREST indication that a suspicious check is a forgery?
    A. There are smudges from carbon paper at the edges of the back of the check.

B. The signature on the check is an exact duplicate of an authentic signature.
C. The amount of the check has been crossed out and a new amount written in.
D. Two different color inks were used in making out the check.

16. Assume an investigator is making an inspection of a desk and finds a writing pad on which a suspect may have written. The top page of the pad has indentations which were formed when the previous page was written on. Following are three procedures which might be appropriate in order to read the indentation:
    I. Hold the paper in such a manner that a single light source falls along the sheet at a parallel or oblique angle.
    II. Soak the pad in water and thoroughly dry it in the sun.
    III. Rub a piece of carbon paper lightly across the underside of the paper in question.
    Which one of the following choices classifies the above statements into those which are APPROPRIATE procedures and those which are NOT APPROPRIATE?
    A. I and II are appropriate, but III is not appropriate
    B. II and III are appropriate, but I is not appropriate
    C. I and III are appropriate, but II is not appropriate
    D. II is appropriate, but I and III are not appropriate

16._____

17. In order to conduct an effective interview, an interviewer's attention must be continuously directed in two ways, toward himself as well as toward the interviewee.
    Of the following, the PRIMARY danger in this division of attention is that the
    A. interviewer's behavior may become less natural and thus alienate the interviewee
    B. interviewee's span of attention will be shortened
    C. interviewer's response may be interpreted by the interviewee as being antagonistic
    D. interviewee's more or less concealed prejudices will come to the surface

17._____

18. X and Y go into a vault together and close the door. A shot is heard, and Y rushes out with a smoking gun in his hand.
    A witness to his event who said *Y shot X* would be offering _____ evidence.
    A. direct   B. real
    C. circumstantial   D. hearsay

18._____

19. Assume that an investigator is attempting to get a suspect to agree to take a lie detector or polygraph test.
    Which of the following actions on the part of the investigator would be LEAST appropriate?
    A. Describe the test to the suspect in simple language so that he understands the procedure
    B. Suggest that the test is a means for the suspect to indicate his innocence

19._____

C. Discuss the test's capability of indicating whether a person is telling the truth
D. Suggest that a refusal to take the test indicates guilt

20. The term *corpus delicti* is MOST appropriately used to refer to
    A. a body of criminal law
    B. the body of a person
    C. a body of civil law
    D. the body of a crime

21. Which of the following is considered the BEST type of permanent ink to use in preparing documents?
    A. Ballpoint
    B. Nigrosine
    C. Log wood
    D. Iron gallotannate

22. An important aspect of investigative work is the preservation of materials which may be used as evidence.
    Following are three statements which might constitute rules for the proper handling of blood in a fluid condition found at a crime scene:
    I. The blood should be removed with an eye dropper and placed in a test tube.
    II. Saline solution should be added to the blood sample in a ratio of 1 to 4.
    III. The sample blood should be frozen and delivered to the laboratory as soon as possible.
    Which of the following choices classifies the above actions into those which are APPROPRIATE and those which are INAPPROPRIATE?
    A. I and II are appropriate, but III is inappropriate.
    B. I and III are appropriate, but II is inappropriate.
    C. I is appropriate, but II and III are inappropriate.
    D. III is appropriate, but I and II are inappropriate.

23. The term *entrapment* refers to the act of
    A. peace officers or agents of the government in inducing a person to commit a crime not contemplated by him for the purpose of instituting a criminal prosecution against him
    B. private individuals inducing a person to commit an act not contemplated by him for the purpose of bringing a civil against him
    C. peace officers or agents of the government in observing a person engaged in the commission of a criminal act and, therefore, obtaining direct evidence against the person
    D. private individuals or investigators in interrupting a person engaged in committing a criminal act

24. Assume you are investigating a person who is alleged to be an officer in a manufacturing corporation doing business in New York City.
    Which of the following sources of information is the LEAST appropriate source to consult in checking whether this is true?
    A. Poor's Register of Directors and Executives
    B. Polk's Banker's Encyclopedia
    C. Moody's Manual of Investments, American and Foreign
    D. Polk's Copartnership and Corporation Directory

25. If an investigator is assigned to the surveillance of a suspect which requires the use of an automobile, it would generally be LEAST advisable for him to use a car
    A. rented from a rental agency
    B. personally owned by the investigator
    C. bearing special unregistered plates
    D. borrowed by someone who is trustworthy but has no official associations

25.____

KEY (CORRECT ANSWERS)

1.	B		11.	B
2.	C		12.	C
3.	D		13.	D
4.	A		14.	A
5.	A		15.	B
6.	D		16.	C
7.	C		17.	A
8.	B		18.	C
9.	A		19.	D
10.	C		20.	D

21.	D
22.	A
23.	A
24.	B
25.	B

TEST 2

DIRECTIONS: Each question or incomplete statement is followed by several suggested answers or completions. Select the one that BEST answers the question or completes the statement. *PRINT THE LETTER OF THE CORRECT ANSWER IN THE SPACE AT THE RIGHT.*

1. Following are three statements regarding writing instruments: 1.____
   I. The hardness of the lead and the sharpness of the point affect the appearance of pencil writing.
   II. The ballpoint pen obscures the writer's ability to exhibit his characteristic habits of quality, rhythm, and shading.
   III. An examination of writing performed with a ballpoint pen easily reveals the angle at which the pen was held with relation to the writer's body and the paper.
   Which of the following choices classifies the above statements into those which are generally CORRECT and those which are generally INCORRECT?
   A. I is correct, but II and III are incorrect.
   B. II is correct, but I and III are incorrect.
   C. I and II are correct, but III is incorrect.
   D. I and III are correct, but II is incorrect.

2. Following are three statements regarding procedures to be followed in obtaining exemplars from a suspect which may or may not be appropriate. 2.____
   I. After the suspect is seated and provided with writing materials, the investigator should dictate the comparison text, always indicating punctuation and paragraphing.
   II. The material should be dictated several times, the speed of the dictation being increased each time so that the suspect will be inclined to lapse into his normal handwriting habits.
   III. As each sheet is completed, it should be removed from the suspect so that he will not be able to imitate the first exemplars he has prepared.
   Which of the following choices classifies the above procedures into those which are APPROPRIATE and those which are INAPPROPRIATE?
   A. I and II are appropriate, but III is inappropriate.
   B. I and III are appropriate, but II is inappropriate.
   C. I is appropriate, but II and III are inappropriate.
   D. III is appropriate, but I and II are inappropriate.

3. During an investigation, it may be necessary to take a *deposition*. 3.____
   The one of the following which BEST describe a *deposition* is
   A. a record made of the case progress
   B. a statement made by a witness in which he agrees to give testimony in court without resort to subpoena
   C. testimony of a witness reduced to writing under oath or affirmation, in answer to interrogatories
   D. another name for an *affidavit*

4. Examination of handwriting on the basis of comparing the outer shapes of letters is known as the _____ method.
   A. holographic   B. penographic   C. calligraphic   D. pedographic

5. An investor who receives a lead from an anonymous phone caller would generally be BEST advised to
   A. ignore the information as unfounded
   B. tell the informant to call back when he is ready to divulge his identity
   C. determine from the informant the motivation behind his making the call
   D. get all relevant information possible on the assumption he will not hear from the caller again

6. In order to demonstrate his findings to the court, a document examiner must use enlarged, mounted photographs.
   Which of the following should ALSO be submitted to the court?
   A. Color enlargements, as well as black and white
   B. Normal-size photographs of the enlarged documents
   C. Negatives of the enlarged photographs
   D. Duplicates of the enlarged photographs

7. X, an investigator, has come upon a few documents belonging to Y, a person whom X is investigating. The documents cannot be taken or moved.
   Of the following, the MOST appropriate action for X to take is to
   A. make a record of the documents, making certain to include any names, addresses, and numbers mentioned even though they may appear meaningless at the time of discovery
   B. make a record only of those documents deemed relevant by him at the time of discover, including names, addresses, and numbers mentioned
   C. leave the documents without making any notes because documents that cannot be moved may not be copied
   D. make a record only of those names, addresses, or numbers mentioned which are clearly relevant to the case

8. Assume that you are interviewing W, a neighbor of N, whom you are investigating. It is important to establish whether or not N uses alcoholic beverages excessively.
   Which of the following questions is MOST appropriate for obtaining the information you seek?
   A. Have you ever seen N intoxicated?
   B. Can you tell me something about N's habits?
   C. Do you know whether or not N is a patron of nearby bars?
   D. What is N's reputation in the neighborhood?

9. A check may be altered to change the amount, the name, or some other element. The one of the following which can BEST be used to discover any changes is
   A. a magnetometer   B. an ultra-violet lamp
   C. a tensimeter   D. polarography

10. Z, an investigator, is attempting to interview W concerning an accident witnessed by W. However, W is disinterested and indifferent.
In order to encourage W's cooperation, Z should
    A. stimulate W's interest by stressing the importance of the information that he possesses
    B. impress upon W that Z is an investigator performing an official function
    C. warn W that the withholding of information may be considered as an obstruction of justice
    D. gain W's sympathy for Z, who is merely trying to do his job

10.____

11. Of the following, the three types of ink MOST commonly used in the United States today are:
    A. gallotannic, logwood, and nigrosine
    B. gallotannic, vanadium, and wolfram
    C. wolfram, logwood, and nigrosine
    D. vanadium, logwood, and nigrosine

11.____

12. Which of the following BEST describes the science of poroscopy? Identification
    A. by the casting of footprints
    B. by the tracing of tools used in a crime
    C. by means of sweat pores indicated on a fingerprint
    D. through the examination of human hairs

12.____

13. Which of the following statements concerning the folding of paper is ACCURATE:
    A. When uncut paper has been folded, the fibers remain unbroken.
    B. If an ink line is first drawn and the paper is subsequently folded, the line over the fold will not be even and uniform.
    C. If an ink line is written over an already existing fold, the ink will spread over the fold but protruding fibers will not become stained.
    D. It is almost impossible to determine whether a lead pencil line was drawn on a paper before or after it was folded.

13.____

14. All of the following are generally good methods of making erased lead-pencil writing visible EXCEPT
    A. examination in non-polarized light   B. use of iodine fumes
    C. contrast photography   D. photography in oblique light

14.____

15. Following are four statements concerning crime-scene photography that may or may not be valid:
    I. The general procedure of crime-scene photography aims at obtaining views of broad areas of the crime locale, supplemented by closer views of sections containing important detail.
    II. The crime scene should be first photographed in its original, undisturbed state.
    III. Crime-scene photographs are of great value to the investigator because they accurately show the distances between objects.

15.____

IV. If a room is to be photographed, a set of at least four views will be required to show the room adequately.

Which of the following choices MOST accurately classifies the above into those which are VALID procedures and those which are NOT VALID?
   A. I and II are valid, but III and IV are not valid.
   B. I, II, and IV are valid, but III is not valid.
   C. III and IV are valid, but I and II are not valid.
   D. I, II, and III are valid, but IV is not valid.

16. Following are four statements concerning the erasing of ink which may or may not be valid:
    I. It may be difficult to detect an erasure made with an eradicator, especially after a considerable length of time has elapsed.
    II. When an erasure has been made with a knife or rubber, it is general easy to detect the area involved, as it is translucent.
    III. The sulfocyanic acid method is inappropriate for the detection of residue of iron-containing inks.
    IV. Examination with ultra-violet rays should not be strongly relied upon because clever forgers have been known to wash away all residue of eradication with distilled water.

    Which of the following choices MOST accurately classifies the above statements into those which are generally VALID and those which are not generally valid?
       A. I and II are generally valid, but III and IV are not generally valid.
       B. IV is generally valid, but I, II, and III are not generally valid.
       C. I, II, and IV are generally valid, but III is not generally valid.
       D. III and IV are generally valid, but I and II are not generally valid.

16.____

17. Following are four statements concerning fingerprints which may or may not be true:
    I. Plastic fingerprints are found on such objects as a bar of soap or ball of melted wax.
    II. Visible fingerprints are left by fingers covered with a colored material such as blood or grease.
    III. The majority of latent fingerprints are relatively invisible and must be developed.
    IV. Dirty surfaces and absorbent materials readily bear prints.

    Which of the following choices MOST accurately classifies the above statements into those which are TRUE and those which are NOT TRUE?
       A. I and II are true; III and IV are not true.
       B. I and III are true; II and IV are not true.
       C. I, II, and III are true, and IV is not true.
       D. I, II, and IV are true, and III is not true.

17.____

18. Of the following, the method of fingerprint classification MOST commonly used in the United States is the _____ system.
    A. Henry   B. Vucetich   C. Bertillon   D. Pottecher

18.____

19. Of the following, the term *curtilage* is MOST appropriately used to refer to
    A. the enclosed space of ground and buildings immediately surrounding a dwelling
    B. a surgical procedure used to induce an abortion
    C. the illegal detention of suspects by law enforcement personnel
    D. a legal action taken by a judge to curtail the irrelevant testimony of witnesses in court

20. Which of the following statements is MOST valid as a guide to investigators in their dealings with informants?
    A. Whether they are agreeable or not, informants should be made available for questioning by other agencies since they may have good information in areas other than those which directly concern you.
    B. Many informants work out of revenge, while some others do it only for money. Therefore, you should evaluate the information they give you with regard to their motivation.
    C. Informants tend to use their connections with law enforcement agencies. From time to time, they must be put in their place by letting them know they are *stool pigeons*.
    D. To cultivate informants, it is a good practice to give them some money in advance so they will be assured of a reward when they have good information.

21. The more meager the evidence against a suspect, the later the suspect should be allowed to know of it.
    As a practical rule to guide the investigator during an interrogation, the advice contained in this statement is GENERALLY
    A. *bad*, chiefly because suspects have a right to know the details of the offense being investigated
    B. *good*, chiefly because the interrogator will not look foolish due to his lack of information
    C. *bad*, chiefly because the investigator will be unable to develop the proper rapport with the suspect during the interrogation
    D. *good*, chiefly because the suspect, not sensing the direction of the interrogation, is more likely to reveal information

22. Following are three statements concerning fingerprinting which may or may not be valid:
    I. The best paper for fingerprinting purposes has a rough surface which will absorb ink.
    II. The subject should roll his fingers on the paper from right to left exercising as much pressure as possible on the paper to make a print.
    III. Fingerprints taken with stamp-pad ink are not usually legible or permanent.
    Which of the following classifies the above statements into those which are VALID and those which are NOT VALID?
    A. I is valid, but II and III are not valid.
    B. I and II are valid, but III is not valid.
    C. II is valid, but I and III are not valid
    D. III is valid, but I and II are not valid.

23. All of the following statements concerning fingerprints are true EXCEPT: 23.____
    A. There are no two identical fingerprints.
    B. Fingerprint patterns are not generally changed by illness.
    C. A modern procedure called dactylmogrification has been developed to change the fingerprints of individuals relatively easily.
    D. If the skin on the fingertips is wounded, the whole fingerprint pattern will reappear when the wound heals.

24. Mechanical erasures on a document produce an abrasion of the paper. Assume that a forger makes an ink writing which crosses an area which has been previously erased. 24.____
    Following are three conditions which might result in the erased area from such an action:
    I. The ink line is brighter.
    II. The ink line is wider.
    III. The ink line tends to run or feather out sideways.
    Which one of the following choices MOST accurately classifies the above statements into those which would result from writing over the erased area and those which would not?
    A. I and II would result, but III would not result.
    B. I and III would result, but I would not result.
    C. II would result, but I and III would not result.
    D. II and III would result, but I would not result.

25. In the investigation of the periodic theft of equipment from stockrooms, the detection of the thieves is USUALLY accomplished by 25.____
    A. the use of strict inventory controls
    B. careful background investigation of applicants for the stockroom jobs
    C. issuing photo identification cards to all employees of the agency
    D. the use of intelligent surveillance

KEY (CORRECT ANSWERS)

1. C	11. A
2. D	12. C
3. C	13. D
4. C	14. A
5. D	15. B
6. B	16. C
7. A	17. C
8. A	18. A
9. B	19. A
10. A	20. B

21. D
22. D
23. C
24. D
25. D

EXAMINATION SECTION
TEST 1

DIRECTIONS: Each question or incomplete statement is followed by several suggested answers or completions. Select the one that BEST answers the question or completes the statement. *PRINT THE LETTER OF THE CORRECT ANSWER IN THE SPACE AT THE RIGHT.*

1. An investigator uses Forms A, B, and C in filling out his investigation reports. He uses Form B five times as often as Form A, and he uses Form C three times as often as Form B.
If the total number of all forms used by the investigator in a month equal 735, how many times was Form B used?
   A. 150   B. 175   C. 205   D. 235

2. Of all the investigators in one agency, 25% work in a particular building. Of these, 12% have desks on the 14th floor.
What percentage of the investigators work in this building but do NOT have desks on the 14th floor?
   A. 12%   B. 13%   C. 22%   D. 23%

3. An investigator is given two reports to read. Report P is 160 pages long and takes the investigator 3 hours and 20 minutes to read.
If Report S is 254 pages long and the investigator reads it at the same rate as he reads Report P, how long will it take him to read Report S? _____ hours _____ minutes.
   A. 4; 15   B. 4; 50   C. 5; 10   D. 5; 30

4. A team of 6 investigators was assigned to interview 234 people.
If half the investigators conduct twice as many interviews as the other half, and the slow group interviews 12 persons a day, how many days would it take to complete this assignment? _____ days.
   A. 4½   B. 5   C. 6   D. 6½

5. The investigators in one agency conduct an average of 12 interviews an hour from 10 A.M. to 12 noon and from 1 P.M. to 5 P.M. daily. The director of his agency knows from past experience that 20% of those called in to be interviewed are unable to keep the appointments that were scheduled.
If the director wants his staff to be kept occupied with interviews for the entire time period that has been set aside for this function, how many appointments should be scheduled for each day?
   A. 86   B. 90   C. 96   D. 101

6. An investigator has a 430-page report to read. The first day, he is able to read 20 pages. The second day, he reads 10 pages more than the first day, and the third day, he reads 15 pages more than the second day.

If, on the following days, he continues to read at the same rate as he was reading on the third day, he will complete the report on the _____ day.
A. 7th B. 8th C. 10th D. 11th

7. The 36 investigators in an agency are each required to submit 25 investigation reports a week. These reports are filled out on a certain form, and only one copy of the form is needed per report.
Allowing 20% for waste, how many packages of 45 forms a piece should be ordered for each weekly period?
A. 15 B. 20 C. 25 D. 30

8. During the fiscal year, an investigative unit received $260 for stationery and telephone expenditures. It spent 43% for stationery and 1/3 of the balance for telephone service.
The amount of money that was left at the end of the fiscal year was MOST NEARLY
A. $49 B. $50 C. $99 D. $109

Questions 9-10.

DIRECTIONS: Questions 9 and 10 are to be answered SOLELY on the data given below.

Number of days absent per worker (sickness)	1	2	3	4	5	6	7	8 or Over
Number of Workers	96	45	16	3	1	0	1	0

Total Number of Workers: 500

9. The TOTAL number of man days lost due to illness in 2020 was
A. 137 B. 154 C. 162 D. 258

10. Of the 500 workers studied, the number who lost NO days due to sickness in 2020 was
A. 230 B. 298 C. 338 D. 372

Questions 11-13.

DIRECTIONS: Questions 11 through 13 are to be answered SOLELY on the basis of the following passage.

The rise of urban-industrial society has complicated the social arrangements needed to regulate contacts between people. As a consequence, there has been an unprecedented increase in the volume of laws and regulations designed to control individual conduct and to govern the relationship of the individual to others. In a century, there has been an eight-fold increase in the crimes for which one may be prosecuted.

For these offenses, the courts have the ultimate responsibility for redressing wrongs and convicting the guilty. The body of legal precepts gives the impression of an abstract and evenhanded dispensation of justice. Actually, the personnel of the agencies applying these precepts are faced with the difficulties of fitting abstract principles to highly variable situations emerging from the dynamics of everyday life. It is inevitable that discrepancies should exist between precept and practice.

The legal institutions serve as a framework for the social order by their slowness to respond to the caprices of transitory fad. This valuable contribution exacts a price in terms of the inflexibility of legal institutions in responding to new circumstances. This possibility is promoted by the changes in values and norms of the dynamic larger culture of which the legal precepts are a part.

11. According to the above passage, the increase in the number of laws and regulations during the twentieth century can be attributed to the
    A. complexity of modern industrial society
    B. increased seriousness of offenses committed
    C. growth of individualism
    D. anonymity of urban living

11.____

12. According to the above passage, which of the following presents a problem to the staff of legal agencies? The
    A. need to eliminate the discrepancy between precept and practice
    B. necessity to apply abstract legal precepts to rapidly changing conditions
    C. responsibility for reducing the number of abstract legal principles
    D. responsibility for understanding offenses in terms of the real-life situations from which they emerge

12.____

13. According to the above passage, it can be concluded that legal institutions affect social institutions by
    A. preventing change
    B. keeping pace with its norms and values
    C. changing its norms and values
    D. providing stability

13.____

Questions 14-16.

DIRECTIONS: Questions 14 through 16 are to be answered SOLELY on the basis of information given in the following passage.

A personnel interviewer, selecting job applicants, may find that he reacts badly to some people even on first contact. This reaction cannot usually be explained by things that the interviewee has done or said. Most of us have had the experience of liking or disliking, of feeling comfortable and uncomfortable with people on first acquaintance, long before we have had a chance to make a conscious, rational decision about them. Often, too, our liking or disliking is transmitted to the other person by subtle processes such as gestures, posture, voice intonations, or choice of words. The point to be kept in mind is this: the relations between people are complex and occur at several levels, from the conscious to the unconscious. This is true whether the relationship is brief or long, formal or informal.

Some of the major dynamics of personality which operate on the unconscious level are projection, sublimation, rationalization, and repression. Encountering these for the first time, one is apt to think of them as representing pathological states. In the extreme, they undoubtedly are, but they exist so universally that we must consider them also to be parts of normal personality.

Without necessarily subscribing to any of the numerous theories of personality, it is possible to describe personality in terms of certain important aspects or elements. We are all aware of ourselves as thinking organisms.

This aspect of personality, the conscious part, is important for understanding human behavior, but it is not enough. Many find it hard to accept the notion that each person also has an unconscious. The existence of the unconscious is no longer a matter of debate. It is not possible to estimate at all precisely what proportion of our total psychological life is conscious, what proportion unconscious. Everyone who has studied the problem, however, agrees that consciousness is the smaller part of personality. Most of what we are and do is a result of unconscious processes. To ignore this is to risk mistakes.

14. The above passage suggests that an interviewer can be MOST effective if he
    A. learns how to determine other peoples' unconscious motivations
    B. learns how to repress his own unconsciously motivated mannerisms and behavior
    C. can keep others from feeling that he either likes or dislikes them
    D. gains an understanding of how the unconscious operates in himself and in others

15. It may be inferred from the above passage that the *subtle processes*, such as gestures, posture, voice intonation, or choice of words referred to in the first paragraph are USUALLY
    A. in the complete control of an expert investigator
    B. the determining factors in the friendships a person establishes
    C. controlled by a person's unconscious
    D. not capable of being consciously controlled

16. The above passage implies that various different personality theories are USUALLY
    A. so numerous and different as to be valueless to an investigator
    B. in basic agreement about the importance of the unconscious
    C. understood by the investigator who strives to be effective
    D. in agreement that personality factors such as projection and repression are pathological

Questions 17-19.

DIRECTIONS: Questions 17 through 19 are to be answered SOLELY on the basis of information contained in the following passage.

No matter how well the interrogator adjusts himself to the witness and how precisely he induces the witness to describe his observations, mistakes still can be made. The mistakes made by an experienced interrogator may be comparatively few, but as far as the witness is concerned, his path is full of pitfalls. Modern "witness psychology" has shown that even the most honest and trustworthy witnesses are apt to make grave mistakes in good faith. It is, therefore, necessary that the interrogator get an idea of the weak links in the testimony in order to check up on them in the event that something appears to be strange or not quite satisfactory.

Unfortunately, modern witness psychology does not yet offer any means of directly testing the credibility of testimony. It lacks precision and method, in spite of worthwhile attempts on the part of learned men. At the same time, witness psychology, through the gathering of many experience concerning the weaknesses of human testimony, has been of invaluable service. It shows clearly that only evidence of a technical nature has absolute value as proof.

Testimony may be separated into the following stages: (1) perception; (2) observation; (3) mind fixation of the observed occurrences, in which fantasy, association of ideas, and personal judgment participate; (4) expression in oral or written form, where the testimony is transferred from one witness to another or to the interrogator. Each of these stages offers innumerable possibilities for the distortion of testimony.

17. The above passage indicates that having witnesses talk to each other before testifying is a practice which is GENERALLY
    A. *desirable*, since the witnesses will be able to correct each other's errors in observation before testimony
    B. *undesirable*, since the witnesses will collaborate on one story to tell the investigator
    C. *undesirable*, since one witness may distort his testimony because of what another witness may erroneously say
    D. *desirable*, since witnesses will become aware of discrepancies in their own testimony and can point out the discrepancies to the investigator

17.____

18. According to the above passage, the one of the following which would be the MOST reliable for use as evidence would be the testimony of a
    A. handwriting expert about a signature on a forged check
    B. trained police officer about the identity of a criminal
    C. laboratory technician about an accident he has observed
    D. psychologist who has interviewed any witness who relate conflicting stories

18.____

19. Concerning the validity of evidence, it is clear from the above passage that
    A. only evidence of a technical nature is at all valuable
    B. the testimony of witnesses is so flawed that it is usually valueless
    C. an investigator, by knowing modern witness psychology, will usually be able to perceive mistaken testimony
    D. an investigator ought to expect mistakes in even the most reliable witness testimony

19.____

Questions 20-21.

DIRECTIONS: Questions 20 and 21 are to be answered SOLELY on the basis of information given in the following passage.

Since we generally assure informants that what they say is confidential, we are not free to tell one informant what the other has told us. Even if the informant says, "*I don't care who knows it; tell anybody you want to*," we find it wise to treat the interview as confidential. An interviewer who relates to some informants what other informants have told him is likely to stir up anxiety and suspicion. Of course, the interviewer may be able to tell an informant what he has heard without revealing the source of his information. This may be perfectly appropriate where a story has wide currency so that an informant cannot infer the source of the information. But if an event is not widely known, the mere mention of it may reveal to one informant what another informant has said about the situation. How can the data be cross-checked in these circumstances.

20. The above passage IMPLIES that the anxiety and suspicion an interviewer may arouse by telling what has been learned in other interviews is due to the   20.____
    A. lack of trust the person interviewed may have in the interviewer's honesty
    B. troublesome nature of the material which the interviewer has learned in other interviews
    C. fact that the person interviewed may not believe that permission was given to repeat the information
    D. fear of the person interviewed that what he is telling the interviewer will be repeated

21. The above passage is MOST likely part of a longer passage dealing with   21.____
    A. ways to verify data gathered in interviews
    B. the various anxieties a person being interviewed may feel
    C. the notion that people sometimes say things they do not mean
    D. ways an interview can avoid seeming suspicious

Questions 22-23.

DIRECTIONS: Questions 22 and 23 are to be answered SOLELY on the basis of information given below.

The ability to interview rests not on any single trait, but on a vast complex of them. Habits, skills, techniques, and attitudes are all involved. Competence in interviewing is acquired only after careful and diligent study, prolonged practice (preferably under supervision), and a good bit of trial and error; for interviewing is not an exact science; it is an art. Like many other arts, however, it can and must draw on science in several of its aspects.

There is always a place for individual initiative, for imaginative innovations, and for new combinations of old approaches. The skilled interviewer cannot be bound by a set of rules. Likewise, there is not a set of rules which can guarantee to the novice that his interviewing will be successful. There are, however, some accepted, general guideposts which may help the beginner to avoid mistakes, learn how to conserve this efforts, and establish effective working relationships with interviewees; to accomplish, in short, what he sets out to do.

22. According to the above passage, rules and standard techniques for interviewing   22.____
    are
    A. helpful for the beginner, but useless for the experienced, innovative interviewer
    B. destructive of the innovation and initiative needed for a good interviewer
    C. useful for even the experienced interviewer who may, however, sometimes go beyond them
    D. the means by which nearly anybody can become an effective interviewer

23. According to the above passage, the one of the following which is a prerequisite   23.____
    to competent interviewing is
    A. avoid mistakes   B. study and practice
    C. imaginative innovation D. natural aptitude

Questions 24-27.

DIRECTIONS: Questions 24 through 27 are to be answered SOLELY on the basis of information given in the following passage.

The question of what material is relevant is not as simple as it might seem. Frequently, material which seems irrelevant to the inexperienced has, because of the common tendency to disguise and distort and misplace one's feelings, considerable significance. It may be necessary to let the client "ramble on" for a while in order to clear the decks, as it were, so that he may get down to things that really are on his mind. On the other hand, with an already disturbed person, it may be important for the interviewer to know when to discourage further elaboration of upsetting material. This is especially the case where the worker would be unable to do anything about it. An inexperienced interviewer might, for instance, be intrigued with the bizarre elaboration of material that the psychotic produces, but further elaboration of this might encourage the client in his instability. A too random discussion may indicate that the interviewee is not certain in what areas the interviewer is prepared to help him, and he may be seeking some direction. Or again, satisfying though it may be for the interviewer to have the interviewee tell him intimate details, such revelations sometimes need to be checked or encouraged only in small doses. An interviewee who has "talked too much" often reveals subsequent anxiety. This is illustrated by the fact that frequently after a "confessional" interview, the interviewee surprises the interviewer by being withdrawn, inarticulate, or hostile, or by breaking the next appointment.

24. Sometimes a client may reveal certain personal information to an interviewer   24.____
    and subsequently may feel anxious about this revelation.
    If, during an interview, a client begins to discuss very personal matters, it would be BEST to
    A. tell the client, in no uncertain terms, that you're not interested in personal details
    B. ignore the client at this point
    C. encourage the client to elaborate further on the details
    D. inform the client that the information seems to be very personal

25. The author indicates that clients with severe psychological disturbances pose an especially difficult problem for the inexperienced interviewer.
The difficulty lies in the possibility of the client
   A. becoming physically violent and harming the interviewer
   B. rambling on for a while
   C. revealing irrelevant details which may be followed by cancelled appointments
   D. reverting to an unstable state as a result of interview material

25.____

26. An interviewer should be constantly alert to the possibility of obtaining clues from the client as to the problem areas.
According to the above passage, a client who discusses topics at random may be
   A. unsure of what problems the interviewer can provide help with
   B. reluctant to discuss intimate details
   C. trying to impress the interviewer with his knowledge
   D. deciding what relevant material to elaborate on

26.____

27. The evaluation of a client's responses may reveal substantial information that may aid the interviewer in assessing the problem areas that are of concern to the client. Responses that seemed irrelevant at the time of the interview may be of significance because
   A. considerable significance is attached to all relevant material
   B. emotional feelings are frequently masked
   C. an initial *rambling on* is often a prelude to what is actually bothering the client
   D. disturbed clients often reveal subsequent anxiety

27.____

Questions 28-30.

DIRECTIONS: Questions 28 through 30 are to be answered SOLELY on the basis of the following passage.

The physical setting of the interview may determine its entire potentiality. Some degree of privacy and a comfortable relaxed atmosphere are important. The interviewee is not encouraged to give much more than his name and address if the interviewer seems busy with other things, if people are rushing about, if there are distracting noises. He has a right to feel that, whether the interview lasts five minutes or an hour, he has, for that time, the undivided attention of the interviewer. Interruptions, telephone calls, and so on, should be reduced to a minimum. If the interviewee has waited in a crowded room for what seems to him an interminably long period, he is naturally in mood to sit down and discuss what is on his mind. Indeed, by that time, the primary thing on his mind may be his irritation at being kept waiting, and he frequently feels it would be impolite to express this. If a wait or interruptions have been unavoidable, it is always helpful to give the client some recognition that these are disturbing and that we can naturally understand that they make it more difficult for him to proceed. At the same time, if he protests that they have not troubled him, the interviewer can best accept his statements at their face value, as further insistence that they must have been disturbing may be interpreted by him as accusing, and he may conclude that the interviewer has been personally hurt by his irritation.

28. Distraction during an interview may tend to limit the client's responses. In a case where an interruption has occurred, it would be BEST for the investigator to
    A. terminate this interview and have it rescheduled for another time period
    B. ignore the interruption since it is not continuous
    C. express his understanding that the distraction can cause the client to feel disturbed
    D. accept the client's protests that he has been troubled by the interruption

29. To maximize the rapport that can be established with the client, an appropriate physical setting is necessary. At the very least, some privacy would be necessary.
    In addition, the interviewer should
    A. always appear to be busy in order to impress the client
    B. focus his attention only on the client
    C. accept all the client's statements as being valid
    D. stress the importance of the interview to the client

30. Clients who have been waiting quite some time for their interview may, justifiably, become upset.
    However, a client may initially attempt to mask these feelings because he may
    A. personally hurt the interviewer
    B. want to be civil
    C. feel that the wait was unavoidable
    D. fear the consequences of his statement

KEY (CORRECT ANSWERS)

1.	B	11.	A	21.	A
2.	C	12.	B	22.	C
3.	D	13.	D	23.	B
4.	D	14.	D	24.	D
5.	B	15.	C	25.	D
6.	D	16.	B	26.	A
7.	C	17.	C	27.	B
8.	C	18.	A	28.	C
9.	D	19.	D	29.	B
10.	C	20.	D	30.	B

TEST 2

DIRECTIONS: Each question or incomplete statement is followed by several suggested answers or completions. Select the one that BEST answers the question or completes the statement. *PRINT THE LETTER OF THE CORRECT ANSWER IN THE SPACE AT THE RIGHT.*

Questions 1-5.

DIRECTIONS: In Questions 1 through 5, choose the statement which is BEST from the point of view of English usage suitable for a business report.

1. A. The client's receiving of public assistance checks at two different addresses were disclosed by the investigation.
    B. The investigation disclosed that the client was receiving public assistance checks at two different addresses.
    C. The client was found out by the investigator to be receiving public assistance checks at two different addresses.
    D. The client has been receiving public assistance checks at two different addresses, disclosed the investigation

    1.____

2. A. The investigation of complaints are usually handled by this unit, which deals with internal security problems in the department.
    B. This unit deals with internal security problems in the department; usually investigating complaints.
    C. Investigating complaints is this unit's job, being that it handles internal security problems in the department
    D. This unit deals with internal security problems in the department and usually investigates complaints.

    2.____

3. A. The delay in completing this investigation was caused by difficulty in obtaining the required documents from the candidate.
    B. Because of difficulty in obtaining the required documents from the candidate is the reason that there was a delay in completing this investigation.
    C. Having had difficulty in obtaining the required documents from the candidate, there was a delay in completing this investigation.
    D. Difficulty in obtaining the required documents from the candidate had the affect of delaying the completion of this investigation.

    3.____

4. A. This report, together with documents supporting our recommendation, are being submitted for your approval.
    B. Documents supporting our recommendation is being submitted with the report for your approval.
    C. This report, together with documents supporting our documentation, is being submitted for your approval.
    D. The report and documents supporting our recommendation is being submitted for your approval.

    4.____

5. A. Several people were interviewed and numerous letters were sent before this case was completed.
    B. Completing this case, interviewing several people and sending numerous letters were necessary.
    C. To complete this case needed interviewing several people and sending numerous letters.
    D. Interviewing several people and sending numerous letters was necessary to complete the case.

Questions 6-20.

DIRECTIONS: For each of the sentences numbered 6 to 20, select from the options given below the MOST applicable choice, and mark your answer accordingly.
  A. The sentence is correct.
  B. The sentence contains a spelling error only.
  C. The sentence contains an English grammar error only.
  D. The sentence contains both a spelling error and an English grammar error.

6. He is a very dependable person whom we expect will be an asset to this division.

7. An investigator often finds it necessary to be very diplomatic when conducting an interview.

8. Accurate detail is especially important if court action results from an investigation.

9. The report was signed by him and I since we conducted the investigation jointly.

10. Upon receipt of the complaint, an inquiry was begun.

11. An employee has to organize his time so that he can handle his workload efficiantly.

12. It was not apparent that anyone was living at the address given by the client.

13. According to regulations, there is to be at least three attempts made to locate the client.

14. Neither the inmate nor the correction officer was willing to sign a formal statement.

15. It is our opinion that one of the persons interviewed were lying.

16. We interviewed both clients and departmental personel in the course of this investigation.

17. It is concievable that further research might produce additional evidence.

18. There are too many occurences of this nature to ignore.

19. We cannot accede to the candidate's request.   19._____

20. The submission of overdue reports is the reason that there was a delay in   20._____
    completion of this investigation.

Questions 21-2.

DIRECTIONS: Each of Questions 21 through 25 consists of three sentences lettered A, B, and
             C. In each of these questions, one of the sentences may contain an error in
             grammar, sentence structure, or punctuation, or all three sentences may be
             correct. If one of the sentences in a question contains an error in grammar,
             sentence structure, or punctuation, print in the space at the right the capital
             letter preceding the sentence which contains the error. If all three sentences
             are correct, print the letter D.

21. A. Mr. Smith appears to be less competent than I in performing these duties.   21._____
    B. The supervisor spoke to the employee, who had made the error, but did
        not reprimand him.
    C. When he found the book lying on the table, he immediately notified the
        owner.

22. A. Being locked in the desk, we were certain that the papers would not be   22._____
        taken.
    B. It wasn't I who dictated the telegram; I believe it was Eleanor.
    C. You should interview whoever comes to the office today.

23. A. The clerk was instructed to set the machine on the table before   23._____
        summoning the manager.
    B. He said that he was not familiar with those kind of activities.
    C. A box of pencils, in addition to erasers and blotters, was included in the
        shipment.

24. A. The supervisor remarked, "Assigning an employee to the proper type of   24._____
        work is not always easy."
    B. The employer found that each of the applicants were qualified to perform
        the duties of the position.
    C. Any competent student is permitted to take this course if he obtains the
        consent of the instructor.

25. A. The prize was awarded to the employee whom the judges believed to be   25._____
        most deserving.
    B. Since the instructor believes this book is the better of the two, he is
        recommending it for use in the school.
    C. It was obvious to the employees that the completion of the task by the
        scheduled date would require their working overtime.

KEY (CORRECT ANSWERS)

1. B
2. D
3. A
4. C
5. A

6. D
7. A
8. A
9. C
10. A

11. B
12. B
13. C
14. A
15. C

16. B
17. B
18. B
19. A
20. C

21. B
22. A
23. B
24. B
25. D

EXAMINATION SECTION
TEST 1

DIRECTIONS: Each question or incomplete statement is followed by several suggested answers or completions. Select the one that BEST answers the question or completes the statement. *PRINT THE LETTER OF THE CORRECT ANSWER IN THE SPACE AT THE RIGHT.*

1. The reliability of information obtained increases with the number of persons interviewed. The more the interviewees differ in their statements, the more persons it is necessary to interview to ascertain the true facts.
   According to this statement, the dependability of the information about an occurrence obtained from interviews is related to
   A. how many people are interviewed
   B. how soon after the occurrence an interview can be arranged
   C. the individual technique of the interviewer
   D. the interviewer's ability to detect differences in the statements of interviewees

1.____

2. A sufficient quantity of the material supplied as evidence enables the laboratory expert to determine the true nature of the substance, whereas an extremely limited specimen may be an abnormal sample containing foreign matter not indicative of the true nature of the material.
   On the basis of this statement alone, it may be concluded that a reason for giving an adequate sample of material for evidence to a laboratory expert is that
   A. a limited specimen spoils more quickly than a larger sample
   B. a small sample may not truly represent the evidence
   C. he cannot analyze a small sample correctly
   D. he must have enough material to keep a part of it untouched to show in court

2.____

Questions 3-4.

DIRECTIONS: Questions 3 and 4 are to be answered SOLELY on the information given in the following paragraph.

    Credibility of a witness is usually governed by his character and is evidenced by his reputation for truthfulness. Personal or financial reasons or a criminal record may cause a witness to give false information to avoid being implicated. Age, sex, physical and mental abnormalities, loyalty, revenge, social and economic status, indulgence in alcohol, and the influence of other persons are some of the many factors which may affect the accuracy, willingness, or ability with which witnesses observe, interpret, and describe occurrences.

3. According to the above paragraph, a witness may, for personal reasons, give wrong information about an occurrence because he

3.____

A. wants to protect his reputation for truthfulness
B. wants to embarrass the investigator
C. doesn't want to embarrass the investigator
D. doesn't really remember what happened

4. According to the above paragraph, factors which influence the witness of an occurrence may affect
   A. not only what he tells about it but what he was able and wanted to see of it
   B. only what he describes and interprets later but not what he actually sees at the time of the event
   C. what he sees but not what he describes
   D. what he is willing to see but not what he is able to see

5. There are few individuals or organizations on whom some records are not kept. This sentence means MOST NEARLY that
   A. a few organizations keep most of the records on individuals
   B. some of the records on a few individuals are destroyed and not kept
   C. there are few records kept on individuals
   D. there is some kind of record kept on almost every individual

Questions 6-10.

DIRECTIONS: Questions 6 through 10 are to be answered SOLELY on the information given in the following paragraph.

Those statutes of limitations which are of interest to a claim examiner are the ones affecting third party actions brought against an insured covered by a liability policy of insurance. Such statutes of limitations are legislative enactments limiting the time within which such actions at law may be brought. Research shows that such periods differ from state to state and vary within the states with the type of action brought. The laws of the jurisdiction in which the action is brought govern and determine the period within which the action may be instituted, regardless of the place of the cause of action or the residence of the parties at the time of cause of action. The period of time set by a statute of limitations for a tort action starts from the moment the alleged tort is committed. The period usually extends continuously until its expiration, upon which legal action may no longer be brought. However, there is a suspension of the running of the period when a defendant has concealed himself in order to avoid service of legal process. The suspension continues until the defendant discontinues his concealment, and then the period starts running again. A defendant may, by his agreement or conduct, be legally barred from asserting the statute of limitations as a defense to an action. The insurance carrier for the defendant may, by the misrepresentation of the claims man, cause such a bar against use of the statute of limitations by the defendant. If the claim examiner of the insurance carrier has by his conduct or assertion lulled the plaintiff into a false sense of security by false representations, the defendant may be barred from setting up the statute of limitations as a defense.

6. Of the following, the MOST suitable title for the above paragraph is:
   A. Fraudulent Use of the Statute of Limitations
   B. Parties at Interest in a Lawsuit
   C. The Claim Examiner and the Law
   D. The Statute of Limitations in Claims Work

7. The period of time during which a third party action may be brought against an insured covered by a liability policy depends on
   A. the laws of the jurisdiction in which the action is brought
   B. where the cause of action which is the subject of the suit took place
   C. where the claimant lived at the time of the cause of action
   D. where the insured lived at the time of the cause of action

8. Time limits in third party actions which are set by the statutes of limitations described above are
   A. determined by claimant's place of residence at start of action
   B. different in a state for different actions
   C. the same from state to state for the same type of action
   D. the same within a state regardless of type of action

9. According to the above paragraph, grounds which may be legally used to prevent a defendant from using the statute of limitations as a defense in the action described are
   A. defendant's agreement or concealment; a charge of liability for death and injury
   B. defendant's agreement or conduct; misrepresentation by the claims man
   C. fraudulent concealment by claim examiner; a charge of liability for death or injury; defendant's agreement
   D. misrepresentation by claim examiner of carrier; defendant's agreement; plaintiff's concealment

10. Suppose an alleged tort was committed on January 1, 2019 and that the period in which action may be taken is set at three years by the statute of limitations. Suppose further that the defendant, in order to avoid service of legal process, had concealed himself from July 1, 2021 through December 2021.
    In this case, the defendant may not use the statute of limitations as a defense unless action is brought by the plaintiff after
    A. January 1, 2022   B. February 28, 2022
    C. June 30, 2022   D. August 1, 2022

Questions 11-15.

DIRECTIONS: Questions 11 through 15 are to be answered SOLELY on the information given in the following paragraph.

The nature of the interview varies with the aim or the use to which it is put. While these uses vary widely, interviews are basically of three types: fact-finding, informing, and motivating. One of these purposes usually predominates in an interview, but not to the exclusion of the other two. If the main purpose is fact-finding, for example, the interviewer must often motivate the interviewee to cooperate in revealing the facts. A major factor in the interview is the interaction of the personalities of the interviewer and the interviewee. The interviewee may not wish to reveal the facts sought; or even though willing enough to impart them, he may not be able to do so because of a lack of clear understanding as to what is wanted or because of lack of ability to put into words the information he has to give. On the other hand, the interviewer may not be able to grasp and report accurately the facts which the one being interviewed is trying to convey. Also, the interviewer's prejudice may make him not want to get at the real facts or make him unable to recognize the truth.

11. According to the above paragraph, the purpose of an interview
    A. determines the nature of the interview
    B. is usually the same for the three basic types of interviews
    C. is predominantly motivation of the interviewee
    D. is usually to check on the accuracy of facts previously obtained

11._____

12. In discussing the use or purpose of an interview, the above paragraph points out that
    A. a good interview should have only one purpose
    B. an interview usually has several uses that are equally important
    C. fact-finding should be the main purpose of an interview
    D. the interview usually has one main purpose

12._____

13. According to the above paragraph, an obstacle to the successful interview sometimes attributable to the interviewee is
    A. a lack of understanding of how to conduct an interview
    B. an inability to express himself
    C. prejudice toward the interviewer
    D. too great a desire to please

13._____

14. According to the above paragraph, one way in which the interviewer may help the interviewee to reveal the facts sought is to
    A. make him willing to impart the facts by stating clearly the consequences of false information
    B. make sure he understands what information is wanted
    C. motivate him by telling him how important he is in the investigation
    D. tell him what words to use to convey the information wanted

14._____

15. According to the above paragraph, bias on the part of the interviewer could
    A. be due to inability to understand the facts being imparted
    B. lead him to report the facts accurately
    C. make the interviewee unwilling to impart the truth
    D. prevent him from determining the facts

15._____

Questions 16-20.

DIRECTIONS: Questions 16 through 20 are to be answered SOLELY on the information given in the following paragraph.

PROCEDURE TO OBTAIN REIMBURSEMENT FROM DEPARTMENT OF HEALTH
FOR CARE OF PHYSICALLY HANDICAPPED CHILDREN

Application for reimbursement must be received by the Department of Health within 30 days of the date of hospital admission in order that the Department of Hospitals may be reimbursed from the date of admission. Upon determination that patient is physically handicapped, as defined under Chapter 780 of the State Laws, the ward clerk shall prepare seven copies of Department of Health Form A-1 or A-2 Application and Authorization and shall submit six copies to the Institutional Collections Unit. The ward clerk shall also initiate two copies of Department of Health Form B-1 or B-2 Financial and Social Report and shall forward them to the Institutional Collections Unit for completion of Page 1 and routing to the Social Service Division for completion of the Social Summary on Page 2. Social Services Division shall return From B-1 or B-2 to the Institutional Collections Unit which shall forward one copy of Form B-1 or B-2 and six copies of Form A-1 or A-2 to Central Office Division of Collections for transmission to Bureau of Handicapped Children, Department of Health.

16. According to the above paragraph, the Department of Health will pay for hospital care for
    A. children who are physically handicapped
    B. any children who are ward patients
    C. physically handicapped adults and children
    D. thirty days for eligible children

17. According to the procedure described in the above paragraph, the definition of what constitutes a physical handicap is made by the
    A. attending physician
    B. laws of the state
    C. Social Services Division
    D. ward clerk

18. According to the above paragraph, Form B-1 or B-2 is
    A. a three-page form containing detachable pages
    B. an authorization form issued by the Department of Hospitals
    C. completed by the ward clerk after the Social Summary has been entered
    D. sent to the Institutional Collections Unit by the Social Service Division

19. According to the above paragraph, after their return by the Social Service Division, the Institutional Collections Unit keeps
    A. one copy of Form A-1 or A-2
    B. one copy of Form A-1 or A-2 and one copy of Form B-1 or B-2
    C. one copy of Form B-1 or B-2
    D. no copies of Forms A-1 or A-2 or B-1 or B-2

20. According to the above paragraph, forwarding the Application and Authorization to the Department of Health is the responsibility of the
    A. Bureau for Handicapped Children
    B. Central Office Division of Collections
    C. Institutional Collections Unit
    D. Social Service Division

21. An investigator interviews members of the public at his desk. The attitude of the public toward this department will probably be LEAST affected by this investigator's
    A. courtesy   B. efficiency   C. height   D. neatness

22. While you are conducting an interview, the telephone at your desk rings.
    Of the following, it would be BEST for you to
    A. ask the interviewer at the next desk to answer your telephone and take the message for you
    B. excuse yourself, pick up the telephone, and tell the person on the other end you are busy and will call him back later
    C. ignore the ringing telephone and continue with the interview
    D. use another telephone to inform the operator not to put calls through to you while you are conducting an interview

23. An interviewee is at your desk, which is quite near to the desks where other people work. He beckons you a little closer and starts to talk in a low voice as though he does not want anyone else to hear him.
    Under these circumstances, the BEST thing for you to do is to
    A. ask him to speak a little louder so that he can be heard
    B. cut the interview short and not get involved in his problems
    C. explain that people at other desks are not eavesdroppers
    D. listen carefully to what he says and give it consideration

24. In the course of your work, you have developed a good relationship with the clerk in charge of the information section of a certain government agency from which you must frequently obtain information. This agency's procedures require that a number of long complicated forms be prepared by you before the information can be released.
    For you to ask the clerk in charge to release information to you without your presenting the forms would be
    A. *unwise*, mainly because the information so obtained is no longer considered official
    B. *wise*, mainly because a great deal of time will be saved by you and by the clerk
    C. *unwise*, mainly because it may impair the good relations you have established
    D. *wise*, mainly because more information can usually be obtained through friendly contacts

25. Sometimes public employees are offered gifts by members of the public in an effort to show appreciation for acts performed purely as a matter of duty. An investigator to whom such a gift was offered refused to accept it.
    The action of the investigator was
    A. *bad*; the gift should have been accepted to avoid being rude to the person making the offer
    B. *bad*; salaries paid public employees are not high enough to justify such refusals

C. *good*; he should accept such a gift only when he has done a special favor for someone
D. *good*; the acceptance of such gifts may raise doubts as to the honesty of the employee

26. From the point of view of current correct English usage and grammar, the MOST acceptable of the following sentences is:
    A. Each claimant was allowed the full amount of their medical expenses.
    B. Either of the three witnesses is available.
    C. Every one of the witnesses was asked to tell his story.
    D. Neither of the witnesses are right.

26.____

27. From the point of view of current correct English usage and grammar, the MOST acceptable of the following sentences is:
    A. Beside the statement to the police, the witness spoke to no one.
    B. He made no statement other than to the police and I.
    C. He made no statement to any one else, aside from the police.
    D. The witness spoke to no one but me.

27.____

28. From the point of view of current correct English usage and grammar, the MOST acceptable of the following sentences is:
    A. The claimant has no one to blame but himself.
    B. The boss sent us, he and I, to deliver the packages.
    C. The lights come from mine and not his car.
    D. There was room on the stairs for him and myself.

28.____

29. Of the following excerpts, selected from letters, the one which is considered by modern letter writing experts to be the BEST is:
    A. Attached please find the application form to be filled out by you. Return the form to this office at the above address.
    B. Forward to this office your check accompanied by the application form enclosed with this letter.
    C. If you wish to apply, please complete and return the enclosed form with your check.
    D. In reply to your letter of December--, enclosed herewith please find the application form you requested.

29.____

30. Which of the following sentences would be MOST acceptable, from the point of view of current correct English usage and grammar, in a letter answering a request for information about eligibility for clinic care?
    A. Admission to this clinic is limited to patients' inability to pay for medical care.
    B. Patients who can pay little or nothing for medical care are treated in this clinic.
    C. The patient's ability to pay for medical care is the determining factor in his admissibility to this clinic.
    D. This clinic is for the patient's that cannot afford to pay or that can pay a little for medical care.

30.____

31. A city employee who writes a letter requesting information from a businessman should realize that, of the following, it is MOST important to
    A. end the letter with a polite closing
    B. make the letter short enough to fit on one page
    C. use a form, such as a questionnaire, to save the businessman's time
    D. use a courteous tone that will get the desired cooperation

31.____

Questions 32-35.

DIRECTIONS: Each of Questions 32 through 35 consists of a sentence which may be classified appropriately under one of the following four categories:
A. incorrect because of faulty grammar or sentence structure
B. incorrect because of faulty punctuation
C. incorrect because of faulty capitalization
D. correct

Examine each sentence carefully. Then, in the corresponding space at the right, print the letter preceding the category which is the BEST of the four suggested above. Each incorrect sentence contains only one type of error. Consider a sentence correct if it contains none of the types of errors mentioned, although there may be other correct ways of expressing the same thought.

32. Despite the efforts of the Supervising mechanic, the elevator could not be started. 32.____

33. The U.S. Weather Bureau, weather record for the accident date was checked. 33.____

34. John Jones accidentally pushed the wrong button and then all the lights went out. 34.____

35. The investigator ought to of had the witness sign the statement. 35.____

Questions 36-55.

DIRECTIONS: Each of Questions 36 through 55 consists of a word in capital letters followed by four suggested meanings of the word. For each question, choose the word or phrase which means MOST NEARLY the same as the word in capital letters.

36. ABUT
    A. abandon   B. assist   C. border on   D. renounce

36.____

37. ABSCOND
    A. draw in   B. give up
    C. refrain from   D. deal off

37.____

38. BEQUEATH
    A. deaden   B. hand down   C. make sad   D. scold

38.____

39. BOGUS
    A. sad   B. false   C. shocking   D. stolen   39.____

40. CALAMITY
    A. disaster   B. female   C. insanity   D. patriot   40.____

41. COMPULSORY
    A. binding   B. ordinary   C. protected   D. ruling   41.____

42. CONSIGN
    A. agree with B. benefit   C. commit   D. drive down   42.____

43. DEBILITY
    A. failure   B. legality   C. quality   D. weakness   43.____

44. DEFRAUD
    A. cheat   B. deny   C. reveal   D. tie   44.____

45. DEPOSITION
    A. absence   B. publication C. removal   D. testimony   45.____

46. DOMICILE
    A. anger   B. dwelling   C. tame   D. willing   46.____

47. HEARSAY
    A. selfish   B. serious   C. rumor   D. unlikely   47.____

48. HOMOGENEOUS
    A. human   B. racial   C. similar   D. unwise   48.____

49. ILLICIT
    A. understood B. uneven   C. unkind   D. unlawful   49.____

50. LEDGER
    A. book of accounts   B. editor
    C. periodical   D. shelf   50.____

51. NARRATIVE
    A. gossip   B. natural   C. negative   D. story   51.____

52. PLAUSIBLE
    A. reasonable   B. respectful
    C. responsible   D. rightful   52.____

53. RECIPIENT
    A. absentee   B. receiver   C. speaker   D. substitute   53.____

54. SUBSTANTIATE
    A. appear for B. arrange   C. confirm   D. combine   54.____

55. SURMISE
    A. aim   B. break   C. guess   D. order

Questions 56-60.

DIRECTIONS: In Questions 56 through 60, one of the four words is misspelled. For each question, choose the word which is misspelled.

56. A. absence   B. accummulate
    C. acknowledgment   D. audible

57. A. benificiary   B. disbursement
    C. exorbitant   D. incidentally

58. A. inoculate   B. liaison   C. acquire   D. noticable

59. A. peddler   B. permissible
    C. persuade   D. pertenant

60. A. reconcilation   B. responsable
    C. sizable   D. substantial

61. Suppose a badly cracked sidewalk, 160 feet long and 14 feet wide, is to be torn up and replaced in four equal sections.
    Each section will have _____ square feet.
    A. 40   B. 220   C. 560   C. 680

62. A businessman pays R dollars a month in rent, has a weekly payroll of P dollars, and a utility bill of U dollars for each two months.
    His annual expenses can be expressed by
    A. 12(R+P+U)   B. 52(R+P+U)
    C. 12(R+52P+6U)   D. 12(R+4P+2U)

63. An interviewer can interview P number of people in H number of hours, including the time needed to prepare a report on each interview.
    The number of people he can interview in a work week of W hours is represented by
    A. HW/P   B. PW/H   C. PH/W   D. 35H/P

64. Claims investigated by a certain unit total $8,430,000 for the year.
    If the cost of investigating these claims is 17.3 cents per $100, the yearly cost of investigating these claims is MOST NEARLY
    A. $1,450   B. $14,500   C. $145,000   D. $1,450,000

65. Suppose that a business you are investigating presents the following figures:

Year	Net Income	Tax Rate on Net Income
2015	$5,500	2%
2016	$5,500	3%
2017	$6,500	2%
2018	$5,200	2½%
2019	$6,200	3%
2020	$6,800	2½%

    According to these figures, it is MOST accurate to say that
    A. less tax was due in 2019 than in 2020
    B. more tax was due in 2015 than in 2018
    C. the same amount of tax was due in 2015 and 2016
    D. the same amount of tax was due in 2017 and 2018

66. In 2020, the number of investigations completed in a certain unit had increased 230 over the number completed in 2019, an increase of 10%. In 2021, the number completed decreased 10% from the number completed in 2020. Therefore, the number of investigations completed in 2021 was _____ the number completed in 2019.
    A. 23 less than
    B. 123 less than
    C. 230 more than
    D. the same as

67. Assume that during a certain period, Unit A investigated 400 cases and Unit B investigated 300 cases.
    If each unit doubled its number of investigations, the proportion of Unit A's investigations to Unit B's investigations would then be _____ it was.
    A. twice what
    B. one-half as large as
    C. one-third larger than
    D. the same as

68. In a certain family, the teenage daughter's annual earnings are 5/8 the earnings of her brother and 1/5 the earnings of her father.
    If her brother earns $19,200 a year, then her father's annual earnings are
    A. $60,000   B. $75,000   C. $80,000   D. $96,000

69. Assume that, of the 1,700 verifications made by a certain investigating unit in a one-week period, 40% were birth records, 30% were military records, 10% were citizenship records, and the remainder were miscellaneous records. Then, the MOST accurate of the following statements about the relative number of different records is that
    A. citizenship records verifications equaled 20% of military record verifications
    B. fewer than 700 verifications were birth records
    C miscellaneous records verifications were 20% more than citizenship records verifications
    D. more than 550 verifications were military records

70. Two units, A and B, answer, respectfully, 1,000 and 1,500 inquiries a month. Assuming that the number of inquiries answered by Unit A increase at the rate of 20 each month, while those answered by Unit B decrease at the rate of 5 each month, the two units will answer the same number of inquiries at the end of _____ months.
    A. 10   B. 15   C. 20   D. 25

71. The interview is only one of the many investigational techniques used by the investigator for gathering information and evidence. Each such technique has its special use.
    The investigator usually finds the interview MOST suitable for getting
    A. facts or leads which are available only through individuals
    B. information available in documents and public records
    C. physical evidence relating to the subject of investigation
    D. information that people hesitate to put into writing

72. An investigator should consult his supervisor on a complicated problem before going ahead with his investigation.
    For an investigator to follow this advice would be
    A. *bad*, mainly because consultation is an admission of the investigator's weakness
    B. *good*, mainly because consultation is likely to lead to additional ideas on how to solve the problem
    C. *bad*, mainly because supervisors don't have time to discuss every problem with each investigator
    D. *good*, mainly because the responsibility for the investigation is shared with the supervisor

73. The general demeanor of the person being interviewed, what he says, and the way in which he says it, will usually give the investigator reliable clues concerning his character.
    It may be concluded from this statement that
    A. investigators usually become well-versed in applied psychology
    B. the behavior of the interviewee may give some indication of his character
    C. the investigator should be particularly on guard against deceit
    D. reliable people always show such reliability in their demeanor

74. Under the city charter, it is incumbent upon the Commissioner of Hospitals to collect for the care and maintenance of a patient in an institution under the jurisdiction of the Department if such patient is able to pay in whole or in part for such care and maintenance.
    According to the preceding statement, it is MOST reasonable to assume that
    A. city hospitals are largely self-sufficient, medical services being donated and operating expenses being derived from income from patients
    B. city hospital facilities are intended for use only by the medically needy
    C. the duty of the Department of Hospitals to charge patients who are able to pay has a legal basis
    D. the majority of patients in city institutions will not willingly pay for their care and consistent efforts must be made to collect

13 (#1)

75. In an experiment, a large group of people witnessed a certain incident. Half of the group was then asked to write a detailed narrative report of what they had seen, while the other half was given a lengthy questionnaire report on the incident to fill out. It was found that the narrative reports covered a greater range of items and contained fewer errors of fact than the question-answer reports.
It is MOST logical to conclude that in this experiment,
  A. narrative report tended to be more accurate than question-answer reports
  B. question-answer reports tended to provide more details, while the narrative reports contained more misstatements of fact
  C. some uncontrolled factor was at work since questionnaires usually elicit much more information than this
  D. the range of questions in the questionnaire was narrow

75.____

76. During the course of an interview, it would be LEAST desirable for the investigator to
  A. correct immediately any grammatical errors made by an interviewee
  B. express himself in such a way as to be clearly understood
  C. restrict the interviewee to the subject of the interview
  D. make notes in a way that will not disturb the interviewee

76.____

77. Municipal hospitals which provide no services for private and semi-private patients shall admit only medically needy persons unless refusal to admit a patient will constitute a hazard to the public health or result in possible danger to the patient's life.
According to this statement, it is MOST logical to assume that
  A. medically needy persons may receive full medical services only in municipal hospitals
  B. no municipal hospitals provide services for private and semi-private patients
  C. services for private and semi-private patients are provided by some municipal hospitals
  D. voluntary and private hospitals provide services only for private and semi-private patients

77.____

78. An investigator is making a neighborhood investigation to find additional witnesses to an automobile accident that happened the day before at a corner in a district of buildings with stores and offices above the stores. He started at 12 noon and stopped at a lunch counter and every store in the vicinity of the accident that was open at the time of the accident.
The investigator's procedure is
  A. *good*; he is likely to find people who were near the scene when the accident happened
  B. *good*; he will find the facts needed in the investigation
  C. *bad*; the investigator should have called first at the offices above the stores, as the view was better from there
  D. *bad*; it is unlikely that people occupied with their business would notice an auto accident outside

78.____

79. An investigator is interviewing a witness who has a speech difficulty. The witness is becoming embarrassed because he has made several errors in telling his story.
Under these circumstances, it would be BEST for the investigator to
   A. call these errors rather sharply to the witness' attention so that he will use greater care in describing the accident
   B. close the interview abruptly in order not to embarrass the witness further
   C. go through the motions of an interview for a while and then close it because this is an unreliable witness
   D. try to ease his embarrassment and help him express himself

80. Some investigators prefer to type a statement to be signed by a witness. Others prefer to write it out in longhand.
One advantage of the handwritten statement as compared with a typewritten statement is that a handwritten statement usually
   A. can be taken immediately while a typed statement cannot
   B. appears to be composed by the witness and so is more reliable
   C. eliminates any future question in court as to who prepared the statement
   D. is not likely to contain as many errors as a statement typed under stress

81. Some testimony cannot be accepted as a fact because the witness could not have perceived personally the events he offers as facts in his testimony.
On this basis, which of the following statements by a witness is MOST acceptable as fact?
   A. "Mr. Brown couldn't hear the horn."
   B. "He intended to call his wife."
   C. "There was no one at his home when he phoned."
   D. "The sidewalk was broken in the spot where he fell."

82. Strategy refers to the general plan or arrangement of the interview; tactics, to what is said or done in the presence of the person being interviewed.
According to this definition, the one of the following which would be an example of interview strategy is
   A. deciding the type of questions to be asked at the interview
   B. maintaining a sincere and reasonable manner
   C. stating the purpose of the interview clearly and simply
   D. wording a question precisely so that there is no misunderstanding as to what is meant

83. The prognosis of the patient's condition is the
   A. description of the patient's present condition
   B. opinion of the major cause of the illness
   C. statement of the expected course of the illness
   D. summary of secondary conditions

84. If a person's employment record indicates that he has never kept a job for any length of time, it is MOST likely that this person is a(n)
   A. part-time worker
   B. trouble maker
   C. unskilled worker
   D. unstable worker

85. In order to help a witness who has had very little education fully understand a statement he is to sign, the investigator, preparing the statement, should
    A. have a notary public witness the preparation and signing of the statement
    B. typewrite the statement since uneducated persons find it hard to read handwritten statements
    C. use legal type questions and answers that are to the point
    D. use the same kind of language that the witness usually speaks

86. Mr. Brown acted out what he had seen happen and described what he was doing by saying, "*Richards was here. The door opened and hit him here—like this.*" The investigator who was recording the interview on tape at his office, said, "*Let me get this straight, Mr. Brown. Richards was standing sideways, two feet from the door, when the door opened, hitting Richard's elbow. Have I got it straight?*" The witness replied, "*Right.*"
    The statement of the investigator under these circumstances was
    A. *bad*; it put words into the mouth of the witness
    B. *bad*; it merely duplicated what the witness had already shown
    C. *good*; it clarified a point that could confuse a listener to the tape
    D. *good*; it showed who was doing the interviewing

87. A significant fact to be remembered by the investigator in the course of his work is that a signed statement by a witness becomes evidence which
    A. can be used later to discredit any major change in the witness's story
    B. cannot be contradicted by other evidence
    C. cannot be used to induce the claimant to agree to a fair settlement
    D. s acceptable in court only if the signer cannot testify in court

88. Which of the following would usually be the BEST question for an investigator to ask a witness to find out what time he got to work?
    A. Did you get to work about 9 o'clock that morning?
    B. I suppose you arrived at the office late that morning?
    C. When did you get to work that day?
    D. You arrived at work late that morning. Can you tell me what time, please?

89. An investigator is examining the application of a 30-year-old applicant for a position.
    Which of the following in his employment history for the past three years would indicate the LEAST need for further investigation of this man's reliability as an employee?
    A. Many changes of employment, each to a position in another state at an equivalent salary
    B. Frequent changes of employment to positions requiring skills the man had never exercised before
    C. Few changes of employment but each change followed by six or more months of unemployment
    D. Few changes of employment, each to a higher salary, with no unemployment

90. Security requirements for employment in defense plants have greatly expanded the number of sources of information about individuals.
   According to the above statement, it is MOST valid to assume that
   A. increased sources of information exist for former defense plant employees
   B. detailed information is available on former defense plant employees
   C. information on former defense plant employees is limited to security information
   D. not much information is available on individuals who never worked in defense plants

90.____

KEY (CORRECT ANSWERS)

1.	A	21.	C	41.	A	61.	C	81.	D
2.	B	22.	B	42.	C	62.	C	82.	A
3.	C	23.	D	43.	D	63.	B	83.	C
4.	A	24.	C	44.	A	64.	B	84.	D
5.	D	25.	D	45.	D	65.	D	85.	D
6.	D	26.	C	46.	B	66.	A	86.	C
7.	A	27.	D	47.	C	67.	D	87.	A
8.	B	28.	A	48.	C	68.	A	88.	C
9.	B	29.	C	49.	D	69.	B	89.	D
10.	C	30.	B	50.	A	70.	C	90.	A
11.	A	31.	D	51.	D	71.	A		
12.	D	32.	C	52.	A	72.	B		
13.	B	33.	B	53.	B	73.	B		
14.	B	34.	D	54.	C	74.	C		
15.	D	35.	A	55.	C	75.	A		
16.	A	36.	C	56.	B	76.	A		
17.	B	37.	D	57.	A	77.	C		
18.	D	38.	B	58.	D	78.	A		
19.	C	39.	B	59.	D	79.	D		
20.	B	40.	A	60.	B	80.	C		

REPORT WRITING

EXAMINATION SECTION

TEST 1

DIRECTIONS: Each question or incomplete statement is followed by several suggested answers or completions. Select the one that BEST answers the question or completes the statement. *PRINT THE LETTER OF THE CORRECT ANSWER IN THE SPACE AT THE RIGHT.*

1. Following are six steps that should be taken in the course of report preparation:
   I. Outlining the material for presentation in the report
   II. Analyzing and interpreting the facts
   III. Analyzing the problem
   IV. Reaching conclusions
   V. Writing, revising, and rewriting the final copy
   VI. Collecting data

   According to the principles of good report writing, the CORRECT order in which these steps should be taken is:
   A. VI, III, II, I, IV, V
   B. III, VI, II, IV, I, V
   C. III, VI, II, I, IV, V
   D. VI, II, III, IV, I, V

   1.____

2. Following are three statements concerning written reports:
   I. Clarity is generally more essential in oral reports than in written reports.
   II. Short sentences composed of simple words are generally preferred to complex sentences and difficult words.
   III. Abbreviations may be used whenever they are customary and will not distract the attention of the reader.

   Which of the following choices correctly classifies the above statements in to those which are valid and those which are not valid?
   A. I and II are valid, but III is not valid
   B. I is valid, but II and III are not valid.
   C. II and III are valid, but I is not valid.
   D. III is valid, but I and II are not valid.

   2.____

3. In order to produce a report written in a style that is both understandable and effective, an investigator should apply the principles of unit, coherence, and emphasis.
   The one of the following which is the BEST example of the principle of coherence is
   A. interlinking sentences so that thoughts flow smoothly
   B. having each sentence express a single idea to facilitate comprehension
   C. arranging important points in prominent positions so they are not overlooked
   D. developing the main idea fully to insure complete consideration

   3.____

4. Assume that a supervisor is preparing a report recommending that a standard work procedure be changed.
Of the following, the MOST important information that he should include in this report is
   A. a complete description of the present procedure
   B. the details and advantages of the recommended procedure
   C. the type and amount of retraining needed
   D. the percentage of men who favor the change

5. When you include in your report on an inspection some information which you have obtained from other individuals, it is MOST important that
   A. this information have no bearing on the work these other people are performing
   B. you do not report as fact the opinions of other individuals
   C. you keep the source of the information confidential
   D. you do not tell the other individuals that their statements will be included in your report

6. Before turning in a report of an investigator of an accident, you discover some additional information you did not know about when you wrote the report. Whether or not you re-write your report to include this additional information should depend MAINLY on the
   A. source of this additional information
   B. established policy covering the subject matter of the report
   C. length of the report and the time it would take you to re-write it
   D. bearing this additional information will have on the conclusions in the report

7. The MOST desirable *first* step in the planning of a written report is to
   A. ascertain what necessary information is readily available in the files
   B. outline the methods you will employ to get the necessary information
   C. determine the objectives and uses of the report
   D. estimate the time and cost required to complete the report

8. In writing a report, the practice of taking up the least important points and the most important points last is a
   A. *good* technique since the final points made in a report will make the greatest impression on the reader
   B. *good* technique since the material is presented in a more logical manner and will lead directly to the conclusions
   C. *poor* technique since the reader's time is wasted by having to review irrelevant information before finishing the report
   D. *poor* technique since it may cause the reader to lose interest in the report and arrive at incorrect conclusions about the report

3 (#1)

9. Which one of the following serves as the BEST guideline for you to follow for effective written reports?
Keep sentences
   A. short and limit sentences to one thought
   B. short and use as many thoughts as possible
   C. long and limit sentences to one thought
   D. long and use as many thoughts as possible

9.____

10. One method by which a supervisor might prepare written reports to management is to begin with the conclusions, results, or summary, and to follow this with the supporting data.
The BEST reason why management may *prefer* this form of report is that
   A. management lacks the specific training to understand the data
   B. the data completely supports the conclusions
   C. time is saved by getting to the conclusions of the report first
   D. the data contains all the information that is required for making the conclusions

10.____

11. When making written reports, it is MOST important that they be
   A. well-worded   B. accurate as to the facts
   C. brief   D. submitted immediately

11.____

12. Of the following, the MOST important reason for a supervisor to prepare good written reports is that
   A. a supervisor is rated on the quality of his reports
   B. decisions are often made on the basis of the reports
   C. such reports take less time for superiors to review
   D. such reports demonstrate efficiency of department operations

12.____

13. Of the following, the BEST test of a good report is whether it
   A. provides the information needed
   B. shows the good sense of the writer
   C. is prepared according to a proper format
   D. is grammatical and neat

13.____

14. When a supervisor writes a report, he can BEST show that he has a understanding of the subject of the report by
   A. including necessary facts and omitting nonessential details
   B. using statistical data
   C. giving his conclusions but not the data on which they are based
   D. using a technical vocabulary

14.____

15. Suppose you and another supervisor on the same level are assigned to work together on a report. You disagree strongly with one of the recommendations the other supervisor wants to include in the report but you cannot change his views.

15.____

Of the following, it would be BEST that
- A. you refuse to accept responsibility for the report
- B. you ask that someone else be assigned to this project to replace you
- C. each of you state his own ideas about this recommendation in the report
- D. you give in to the other supervisor's opinion for the sake of harmony

16. Standardized forms are often provided for submitting reports. 16.____
Of the following, the MOST important advantage of using standardized forms for reports is that
    - A. they take less time to prepare than individually written reports
    - B. the person making the report can omit information he considers unimportant
    - C. the responsibility for preparing these reports can be turned over to subordinates
    - D. necessary information is less likely to be omitted

17. A report which may BEST be classed as a *periodic* report is one which 17.____
    - A. requires the same type of information at regular intervals
    - B. contains detailed information which is to be retained in permanent records
    - C. is prepared whenever a special situation occurs
    - D. lists information in graphic form

18. In the writing of reports or letters, the ideas presented in a paragraph are usually 18.____
of unequal importance and require varying degrees of emphasis.
All of the following are methods of placing extra stress on an idea EXCEPT
    - A. repeating it in a number of forms
    - B. placing it in the middle of the paragraph
    - C. placing it either at the beginning or at the end of a paragraph
    - D. underlining it

Questions 19-25.

DIRECTIONS: Questions 19 through 25 concern the subject of report writing and are based on the information and incidents described in the following paragraph. (In answering these questions, assume that the facts and incidents in the paragraph are true.)

On December 15, at 8 A.M., seven Laborers reported to Foreman Joseph Meehan in the Greenbranch Yard in Queens. Meehan instructed the men to load some 50-pound boxes of books on a truck for delivery to an agency building in Brooklyn. Meehan told the men that, because the boxes were rather heavy, two men should work together, helping each other lift and load each box. Since Michael Harper, one of the Laborers, was without a partner, Meehan helped him with the boxes for a while. When Meehan was called to the telephone in a nearby building, however, Harper decided to lift a box himself. He appeared able to lift the box, but, as he got the box halfway up, he cried out that he had a sharp pain in his back. Another Laborer, Jorge Ortiz, who was passing by, ran over to help Harper put the box down. Harper suddenly dropped the box, which fell on Ortiz' right foot. By this time, Meehan had come out of the building. He immediately helped get the box off Ortiz' foot and had both men lie down. Meehan covered the men with blankets and called an ambulance, which arrived a half hour later. At the hospital, the doctor said that the X-ray results showed that Ortiz' right foot was broken in three places.

19. What would be the BEST term to use in a report describing the injury of Jorge Ortiz?
    A. Strain   B. Fracture   C. Hernia   D. Hemorrhage

    19._____

20. Which of the following would be the MOST accurate summary for the Foreman to put in his report of the incident?
    A. Ortiz attempted to help Harper carry a box which was too heavy for one person, but Harper dropped it before Ortiz got there.
    B. Ortiz tried to help Harper carry a box but Harper got a pain in his back and accidentally dropped the box on Ortiz' foot.
    C. Harper refused to follow Meehan's orders and lifted a box too heavy for him; he deliberately dropped it when Ortiz tried to help him carry it.
    D. Harper lifted a box and felt a pain in his back; Ortiz tried to help Harper put the box down but Harper accidentally dropped it on Ortiz' foot.

    20._____

21. One of the Laborers at the scene of the accident was asked his version of the incident.
    Which information obtained from this witness would be LEAST important for including in the accident report?
    A. His opinion as to the cause of the accident
    B. How much of the accident he saw
    C. His personal opinion of the victims
    D. His name and address

    21._____

22. What should be the MAIN objective of writing a report about the incident described in the above paragraph? To
    A. describe the important elements in the accident situation
    B. recommend that such Laborers as Ortiz be advised not to interfere in another's work unless given specific instructions
    C. analyze the problems occurring when there are not enough workers to perform a certain task
    D. illustrate the hazards involved in performing routine everyday tasks

    22._____

23. Which of the following is information *missing* from the above passage but which *should* be included in a report of the incident? The
    A. name of the Laborer's immediate supervisor
    B. contents of the boxes
    C. time at which the accident occurred
    D. object or action that caused the injury to Ortiz' foot

    23._____

24. According to the description of the incident, the accident occurred because
    A. Ortiz attempted to help Harper who resisted his help
    B. Harper failed to follow instructions given him by Meehan
    C. Meehan was not supervising his men as closely as he should have
    D. Harper was not strong enough to carry the box once he lifted it

    24._____

25. Which of the following is MOST important for a foreman to avoid when writing up an official accident report?
    A. Using technical language to describe equipment involved in the accident
    B. Putting in details which might later be judged unnecessary
    C. Giving an opinion as to conditions that contributed to the accident
    D. Recommending discipline for employees who, in his opinion, caused the accident

KEY (CORRECT ANSWERS)

1.	B		11.	B
2.	C		12.	B
3.	A		13.	A
4.	B		14.	A
5.	B		15.	C
6.	D		16.	D
7.	C		17.	A
8.	D		18.	B
9.	A		19.	B
10.	C		20.	D

21. C
22. A
23. C
24. B
25. D

TEST 2

DIRECTIONS: Each question or incomplete statement is followed by several suggested answers or completions. Select the one that BEST answers the question or completes the statement. *PRINT THE LETTER OF THE CORRECT ANSWER IN THE SPACE AT THE RIGHT.*

1. Lieutenant X is preparing a report to submit to his commanding officer in order to get approval of a plan of operation he has developed.
   The report starts off with the statement of the problem and continues with the details of the problem. It contains factual information gathered with the help of field and operational personnel. It contains a final conclusion and recommendation for action. The recommendation is supplemented by comments from other precinct staff members on how the recommendations will affect their areas of responsibility. The report also includes directives and general orders ready for the commanding officer's signature. In addition, it has two statements of objections presented by two precinct staff members.
   Which one of the following, if any, is either an item that Lieutenant X should have included in his report and which is not mentioned above, or is an item which Lieutenant X improperly did include in his report?
   A. Considerations of alternative courses of action and their consequences should have been covered in the report.
   B. The additions containing undocumented objections to the recommended course of action should not have been included as part of the report.
   C. A statement on the qualifications of Lieutenant X, which would support his expertness in the field under consideration, should have been included in the report.
   D. The directives and general orders should not have been prepared and included in the report until the commanding officer had approved the recommendations.
   E. None of the above, since Lieutenant X's report was both proper and complete.

   1.____

2. During a visit to a section, the district supervisor criticizes the method being used by the assistant foreman to prepare a certain report and orders him to modify the method. This change ordered by the district supervisor is in direct conflict with the specific orders of the foreman.
   In this situation, it would be BEST for the assistant foreman to
   A. change the method and tell the foreman about the change at the first opportunity
   B. change the method and rely on the district supervisor to notify the foreman
   C. report the matter to the foreman and delay the preparation of the report
   D. ask the district supervisor to discuss the matter with the foreman but use the old method for the time being

   2.____

3. A department officer should realize that the MOST usual reason for writing a report is to
   A. give orders and follow up their execution
   B. establish a permanent record
   C. raise questions
   D. supply information

4. A very important report which is being prepared by a department officer will soon be due on the desk of the district supervisor. No typing help is available at this time for the officer.
   For the officer to write out this report in longhand in such a situation would be
   A. *bad*; such a report would not make the impression a typed report would
   B. *good*; it is important to get the report in on time
   C. *bad*; the district supervisor should not be required to read longhand reports
   D. *good*; it would call attention to the difficult conditions under which this section must work

5. In a well-written report, the length of each paragraph in the report should be
   A. varied according to the content
   B. not over 300 words
   C. pretty nearly the same
   D. gradually longer as the report is developed and written

6. A clerk in the headquarters office complains to you about the way in which you are filing out a certain report.
   It would be BEST for you to
   A. tell the clerk that you are following official procedures in filling out the report
   B. ask to be referred to the clerk's superior
   C. ask the clerk exactly what is wrong with the way in which you are filling out the report
   D. tell the clerk that you are following the directions of the district supervisor

7. The use of an outline to help in writing a report is
   A. *desirable*, in order to insure good organization and coverage
   B. *necessary*, so it can be used as an introduction to the report itself
   C. *undesirable*, since it acts as a straightjacket and may result in an unbalanced report
   D. *desirable*, if you know your immediate supervisor reads reports with extreme care and attention

8. It is advisable that a department officer do his paper work and report writing as soon as he has completed an inspection MAINLY because
   A. there are usually deadlines to be met
   B. it insures a steady work-flow
   C. he may not have time for this later
   D. the facts are then freshest in his mind

9. Before you turn in a report you have written of an investigation that you have made, you discover some additional information you didn't know about before. Whether or not you re-write the report to include this additional information should depend MAINLY on the
    A. amount of time remaining before the report is due
    B. established policy of the department covering the subject matter of the report
    C. bearing this information will have on the conclusions of the report
    D. number of people who will eventually review the report

9.____

10. When a supervisory officer submits a periodic report to the district supervisor, he should realize that the CHIEF importance of such a report is that it
    A. is the principal method of checking on the efficiency of the supervisor and his subordinates
    B. is something to which frequent reference will be made
    C. eliminates the need for any personal follow-up or inspection by higher echelons
    D. permits the district supervisor to exercise his functions of direction, supervision, and control better

10.____

11. Conclusions and recommendations are usually placed at the end rather than at the beginning of a report because
    A. the person preparing the report may decide to change some of the conclusions and recommendations before he reaches the end of the report
    B. they are the most important part of the report
    C. they can be judged better by the person to whom the report is sent after he reads the facts and investigators which come earlier in the report
    D. they can be referred to quickly when needed without reading the rest of the report

11.____

12. The use of the same method of record-keeping and reporting by all agency sections is
    A. *desirable*, MAINLY because it saves time in section operations
    B. *undesirable*, MAINLY because it kills the initiative of the individual section foreman
    C. *desirable*, MAINLY because it will be easier for the administrator to evaluate and compare section operations
    D. *undesirable*, MAINLY because operations vary from section to section and uniform record-keeping and reporting is not appropriate

12.____

13. The GREATEST benefit the section officer will have from keeping complete and accurate records and reports of section operations is that
    A. he will find it easier to run his section efficiently
    B. he will need less equipment
    C. he will need less manpower
    D. the section will run smoothly when he is out

13.____

14. You have prepared a report to your superior and are ready to send it forward. But on re-reading it, you think some parts are not clearly expressed and your superior ay have difficulty getting your point.
    Of the following, it would be BEST for you to
    A. give the report to one of your men to read, and if he has no trouble understanding it send it through
    B. forward the report and call your superior the next day to ask whether it was all right
    C. forward the report as is; higher echelons should be able to understand any report prepared by a section officer
    D. do the report over, re-writing the sections you are in doubt about

14.____

15. The BEST of the following statements concerning reports is that
    A. a carelessly written report may give the reader an impression of inaccuracy
    B. correct grammar and English are unimportant if the main facts are given
    C. every man should be required to submit a daily work report
    D. the longer and more wordy a report is, the better it will read

15.____

16. In writing a report, the question of whether or not to include certain material could be determined BEST by considering the
    A. amount of space the material will occupy in the report
    B. amount of time to be spent in gathering the material
    C. date of the material
    D. value of the material to the superior who will read the report

16.____

17. Suppose you are submitting a fairly long report to your superior.
    The one of the following sections that should come FIRST in this report is a
    A. description of how you gathered material
    B. discussion of possible objections to your recommendations
    C. plan of how your recommendations can be put into practice
    D. statement of the problem dealt with

17.____

Questions 18-20.

DIRECTIONS: A foreman is asked to write a report on the incident described in the following passage. Answer Questions 18 through 20 based on the following information.

On March 10, Henry Moore, a laborer, was in the process of transferring some equipment from the machine shop to the third floor. He was using a dolly to perform this task and, as he was wheeling the material through the machine shop, laborer Bob Greene called to him. As Henry turned to respond to Bob, he jammed the dolly into Larry Mantell's leg, knocking Larry down in the process and causing the heavy drill that Larry was holding to fall on Larry's foot. Larry started rubbing his foot and then, infuriated, jumped up and punched Henry in the jaw. The force of the blow drove Henry's head back against the wall. Henry did not fight back; he appeared to be dazed. An ambulance was called to take Henry to the hospital, and the ambulance attendant told the foreman that it appeared likely that Henry had suffered a concussion. Larry's injuries consisted of some bruises, but he refused medical attention.

18. An adequate report of the above incident should give as minimum information the names of the persons involved, the names of the witnesses, the date and the time that each event took place, and the
    A. names of the ambulance attendants
    B. names of all the employees working in the machine shop
    C. location where the accident occurred
    D. nature of the previous safety training each employee had been given

    18.____

19. The only one of the following which is NOT a fact is
    A. Bob called to Henry
    B. Larry suffered a concussion
    C. Larry rubbed his foot
    D. the incident took place in the machine shop

    19.____

20. Which of the following would be the MOST accurate summary of the incident for the foreman to put in his report of the accident?
    A. Larry Mantell punched Henry Moore because a drill fell on his foot and he was angry. Then Henry fell and suffered a concussion.
    B. Henry Moore accidentally jammed a dolly into Larry Mantell's foot, knocking Larry down. Larry punched Henry, pushing him into the wall and causing him to bang his head against the wall.
    C. Bob Greene called Henry Moore. A dolly than jammed into Larry Mantell and knocked him down. Larry punched Henry who tripped and suffered some bruises. An ambulance was called.
    D. A drill fell on Larry Mantell's foot. Larry jumped up suddenly and punched Henry Moore and pushed him into the wall. Henry may have suffered a concussion as a result of falling.

    20.____

Questions 21-25.

DIRECTIONS: Questions 21 through 25 are to be answered ONLY on the basis of the information provided in the following passage.

A written report is a communication of information from one person to another. It is an account of some matter especially investigated, however routine that matter may be. The ultimate basis of any good written report is facts, which become known through observation and verification. Good written reports may seem to be no more than general ideas and opinions. However, in such cases, the facts leading to these opinions were gathered, verified, and reported earlier, and the opinions are dependent upon these facts. Good style, proper form, and emphasis cannot make a good written report out of unreliable information and bad judgment; but, on the other hand, solid investigation and brilliant thinking are not likely to become very useful until they are effectively communicated to others. If a person's work calls for written reports, then his work is often no better than his written reports.

21. Based on the information in the above passage, it can be concluded that opinions expressed in a report should be
    A. based on facts which are gathered and reported
    B. emphasized repeatedly when they result from a special investigation
    C. kept to a minimum
    D. separated from the body of the report

22. In the above passage, the one of the following which is mentioned as a way of establishing facts is
    A. authority
    B. communication
    C. reporting
    D. verification

23. According to the above passage, the characteristic shared by ALL written reports is that they are
    A. accounts of routine matters
    B. transmissions of information
    C. reliable and logical
    D. written in proper form

24. Which of the following conclusions can logically be drawn from the information given in the above passage?
    A. Brilliant thinking can make up for unreliable information in a report.
    B. One method of judging an individual's work is the quality of the written reports he is required to submit.
    C. Proper form and emphasis can make a good report out of unreliable information.
    D. Good written reports that seem to be no more than general ideas should be rewritten.

25. Which of the following suggested titles would be MOST appropriate for this passage?
    A. Gathering and Organizing Facts
    B. Techniques of Observation
    C. Nature and Purpose of Reports
    D. Reports and Opinions: Differences and Similarities

KEY (CORRECT ANSWERS)

1. A
2. A
3. D
4. B
5. A

6. C
7. A
8. D
9. C
10. D

11. C
12. C
13. A
14. D
15. A

16. D
17. D
18. C
19. B
20. B

21. A
22. D
23. B
24. B
25. C

TEST 3

DIRECTIONS: Each question or incomplete statement is followed by several suggested answers or completions. Select the one that BEST answers the question or completes the statement. *PRINT THE LETTER OF THE CORRECT ANSWER IN THE SPACE AT THE RIGHT.*

Questions 1-5.

DIRECTIONS: The following is an accident report similar to those used in departments for reporting accidents. Questions 1 through 5 are be answered using ONLY the information given in this report.

ACCIDENT REPORT

FROM: John Doe	DATE OF REPORT: June 23	
TITLE: Sanitation Worker		
DATE OF ACCIDENT: June 22 time 3 ~~AM~~ PM	CITY: Metropolitan	
PLACE: 1489 Third Avenue		
VEHICLE NO. 1	VEHICLE NO. 2	
OPERATOR: John Doe, Sanitation Worker Title	OPERATOR: Richard Roe	
VEHICLE CODE NO: 14-238	ADDRESS: 498 High Street	
LICENSE NO.: 0123456	OWNER: Henry Roe ADDRESS: 786 E.83 St.	LIC. NO.: 5N1492
DESCRIPTION OF ACCIDENT: Light green Chevrolet sedan while trying to pass drove in to rear side of sanitation truck which had stopped to collect garbage. No one was injured but there was property damage.		
NATURE OF DAMAGE TO PRIVATE VEHICLE: Right front fender crushed, bumper bent		
DAMAGE TO CITY VEHICLE: Front of left rear fender pushed in. Paint scraped.		
NAME OF WITNESS: Frank Brown	ADDRESS: 48 Kingsway	
SIGNATURE OF PERSON MAKING THIS REPORT *John Doe*	BADGE NO.: 428	

1. Of the following, the one which has been omitted from this accident report is the
   A. location of the accident
   B. drivers of the vehicles involved
   C. traffic situation at the time of the accident
   D. owners of the vehicles involved

2. The address of the driver of Vehicle No. 1 is not required because he
   A. is employed by the department
   B. is not the owner of the vehicle
   C. reported the accident
   D. was injured in the accident

3. The report indicates that the driver of Vehicle No. 2 was PROBABLY
   A. passing on the wrong side of the truck
   B. not wearing his glasses
   C. not injured in the accident
   D. driving while intoxicated

2 (#3)

4. The number of people *specifically* referred to in this report is
   A. 3   B. 4   C. 5   D. 6

   4.____

5. The license number of Vehicle No. 1 is
   A. 428   B. 5N1492   C. 14-238   D. 0123456

   5.____

6. In a report of unlawful entry into department premises, it is LEAST important to include the
   A. estimated value of the property missing
   B. general description of the premises
   C. means used to get into the premises
   D. time and date of entry

   6.____

7. In a report of an accident, it is LEAST important to include the
   A. name of the insurance company of the person injured in the accident
   B. probable cause of the accident
   C. time and place of the accident
   D. names and addresses of all witnesses of the accident

   7.____

8. Of the following, the one which is NOT required in the preparation of a weekly functional expense report is the
   A. hourly distribution of the time by proper heading in accordance with the actual work performed
   B. signatures of officers not involved in the preparation of the report
   C. time records of the men who appear on the payroll of the respective locations
   D. time records of men working in other districts assigned to this location

   8.____

KEY (CORRECT ANSWERS)

1.	C	5.	D
2.	A	6.	B
3.	C	7.	A
4.	B	8.	B

INTERVIEWING
EXAMINATION SECTION
TEST 1

DIRECTIONS: Each question or incomplete statement is followed by several suggested answers or completions. Select the one that BEST answers the question or completes the statement. *PRINT THE LETTER OF THE CORRECT ANSWER IN THE SPACE AT THE RIGHT.*

1. Of the methods given below for obtaining desired information from applicants, the one considered the BEST interviewing method is to
    A. work from an outline, asking the questions in the order in which they appear and requiring the applicant to give specific answers
    B. let the applicant tell what he has to say in his own way first, the interviewer then taking responsibility for asking questions on points not covered
    C. tell the applicant all the facts that it is necessary to have, then letting him give the information in any way he chooses
    D. verify all such facts as birth date, income, and past employment before seeing the applicant, then asking the applicant to fill in the remaining gaps when he is interviewed

1._____

2. Suppose an applicant objects to answering a question regarding his recent employment and asks, "What business is it of yours, young man?"
In conducting the interview, the MOST constructive course of action for you to take under the circumstances would be to
    A. tell the applicant you have no intention of prying into his personal affairs and go on to the next question
    B. refer the applicant to your supervisor
    C. rephrase the question so that only a "Yes" or "No" answer is required
    D. explain why the question is being asked

2._____

3. An interview is BEST conducted in private PRIMARILY because
    A. the person interviewed will tend to be less self-conscious
    B. the interviewer will be able to maintain his continuity of thought better
    C. it will insure that the interview is "off the record"
    D. people tend to "show off" before an audience

3._____

4. An interviewer will be better able to understand the person interviewed and his problems if he recognizes that much of the person's behavior is due to motives
    A. which are deliberate
    B. of which he is unaware
    C. which are inexplicable
    D. which are kept under control

4._____

5. When an applicant is repeatedly told that "everything will be all right," the effect that can USUALLY be expected is that he will
   A. develop overt negativistic reactions toward the agency
   B. become too closely identified with the interviewer
   C. doubt the interviewer's ability to understand and help with his problems
   D. have greater confidence in the interviewer

6. While interviewing a client, it is PREFERABLE that the interviewer
   A. take no notes in order to avoid disturbing the client
   B. focus primary attention on the client while the client is talking
   C. take no notes in order to impress upon the client the interviewer's ability to remember all the pertinent facts of his case
   D. record all the details in order to show the client that what he says is important

7. During an interview, a curious applicant asks several questions about the interviewer's private life.
   As the interviewer, you should
   A. refuse to answer such questions
   B. answer his questions fully
   C. explain that your primary concern is with his problems and that discussion of your personal affairs will not be helpful in meeting his needs
   D. explain that it is the responsibility of the interviewer to ask questions and not to answer them

8. An interviewer can BEST establish a good relationship with the person being interviewed by
   A. assuming casual interest in the statements made by the person being interviewed
   B. asking questions which enable the person to show pride in his knowledge
   C. taking the point of view of the person interviewed
   D. showing a genuine interest in the person

9. An interviewer's attention must be directed toward himself as well as toward the person interviewed.
   This statement means that the interviewer should
   A. keep in mind the extent to which his own prejudices may influence his judgment
   B. rationalize the statements made by the person interviewed
   C. gain the respect and confidence of the person interviewed
   D. avoid being too impersonal

10. More complete expression will be obtained from a person being interviewed if the interviewer can create the impression that
    A. the data secured will become part of a permanent record
    B. official information must be accurate in every detail
    C. it is the duty of the person interviewed to give accurate data
    D. the person interviewed is participating in a discussion of his own problems

11. The practice of asking leading questions should be avoided in an interview because the
    A. interviewer risks revealing his attitudes to the person being interviewed
    B. interviewer may be led to ignore the objective attitudes of the person interviewed
    C. answers may be unwarrantedly influenced
    D. person interviewed will resent the attempt to lead him and will be less cooperative

11.____

12. A good technique for the interviewer to use in an effort to secure reliable data and to reduce the possibility of misunderstanding is to
    A. use casual undirected conversation, enabling the person being interviewed to talk about himself, and thus secure the desired information
    B. adopt the procedure of using direct questions regularly
    C. extract the desired information from the person being interviewed by putting him on the defensive
    D. explain to the person being interviewed the information desired and the reason for needing it

12.____

13. In interviewing an applicant, your attitude toward his veracity should be that the information he has furnished you is
    A. *untruthful* until you have had an opportunity to check the information
    B. *truthful* only insofar as verifiable facts are concerned
    C. *untruthful* because clients tend to interpret everything in their own favor
    D. *truthful* until you have information to the contrary

13.____

14. When an agency assigns its most experienced interviewers to conduct initial interviews with applicants, the MOST important reason for its action is that
    A. experienced workers are always older and, therefore, command the respect of applicants
    B. the applicant may be given a complete understanding of the procedures to be followed and the time involved in obtaining assistance
    C. applicants with fraudulent intentions will be detected, and prevented from obtaining further services from the agency
    D. the applicant may be given an understanding of the purpose of the assistance program and of the bases for granting assistance, in addition to the routine information

14.____

15. In conducting the first interview with an applicant, you should
    A. ask questions requiring "Yes" or "No" answers in order to simplify the interview
    B. rephrase several of the key questions as a check on his previous statements
    C. let him tell his own story while keeping him to the relevant facts
    D. avoid showing any sympathy for the applicant while he is revealing his personal needs and problems

15.____

16. When an interview opens an interview by asking the client direct questions about his work, it is very likely that the client will feel
    A. that the interview is interested in him
    B. at ease if his work has been good
    C. free to discuss his attitudes toward his work
    D. that good reports are of great importance to the interviewer in his thinking

17. When an interviewer does NOT understand the meaning of a response that a client has made, the interviewer should
    A. proceed to another topic
    B. state that he does not understand and ask for clarification
    C. act as if he understands so that the client's confidence in him should not be shaken
    D. ask the client to rephrase his response

18. When an interviewer makes a response which brings on a high degree of resistance in the client, he should
    A. apologize and rephrase his remark in a less evocative manner
    B. accept the resistance on the part of the client
    C. ignore the client's resistance
    D. recognize that little more will be accomplished in the interview and suggest another appointment

19. Most definitions of interviewing would NOT include the following as a necessary aspect:
    A. The interviewer and client meet face-to-face and talk things out
    B. The client is experiencing considerable emotional disturbance
    C. A valuable learning opportunity is provided for the client
    D. The interviewer brings a special competence to the relationship

20. A powerful dynamic in the interviewing process and often the very *antonym* of its counterpart in the instructional process is
    A. encouraging accuracy
    B. emphasizing structure
    C. pointing up sequential and orderly thinking
    D. processing ambiguity and equivocation

21. Interviewing techniques are frequently useful in working with clients.
    A basic fundamental is an atmosphere which may BEST be described as
    A. non-threatening
    B. motivating for creativity
    C. highly charged to stimulate excitement
    D. fairly-well structured

22. In interviewing the disadvantaged client, the subtle technique of steering away from high-level educational and vocational plans must be *replaced* by
    A. a wait-and-see explanation to the client
    B. the use of prediction tables to determine possibilities and probabilities of overcoming this condition

C. avoidance in discussing controversial issues of deprivation
D. encouragement and concrete consideration for planning his future

23. The process of collecting, analyzing, synthesizing, and interpreting information about the client should be
    A. completed prior to interviewing
    B. completed early in the interviewing process
    C. limited to a type of interviewing which is primarily diagnostic in purpose
    D. continuously pursued throughout interviewing

23.____

24. Catharsis, the "emotional unloading" of the client's feelings, has a value in the early stages of interviewing because it accomplishes all BUT which one of the following goals?
    It
    A. relieves strong physiological tensions in the client
    B. increases the client's anxiety and aggrandizes his motivation to continue counseling
    C. provides a strong substitute for "acting out" the client's feelings
    D. releases emotional energy which the client has been using to bulwark his defenses

24.____

25. In the interviewing process, the interviewer should *usually* give information
    A. whenever it is needed
    B. at the end of the process
    C. in the introductory interview
    D. just before the client would ordinarily request it

25.____

KEY (CORRECT ANSWERS)

1.	B	11.	C
2.	D	12.	D
3.	A	13.	D
4.	B	14.	D
5.	C	15.	C
6.	B	16.	D
7.	C	17.	B
8.	D	18.	B
9.	A	19.	B
10.	D	20.	D

21. A
22. D
23. D
24. B
25. A

TEST 2

DIRECTIONS: Each question or incomplete statement is followed by several suggested answers or completions. Select the one that BEST answers the question or completes the statement. *PRINT THE LETTER OF THE CORRECT ANSWER IN THE SPACE AT THE RIGHT.*

1. Of the following problems that might affect the conduct and outcome of an interview, the MOST troublesome and usually the MOST difficult for the interviewer to control is the
    A. tendency of the interviewee to anticipate the needs and preferences of the interviewer
    B. impulse to cut the interviewee off when he seems to have reached the end of an idea
    C. tendency of interviewee attitude to bias the results
    D. tendency of the interviewer to do most of the talking

2. The supervisor MOST likely to be a good interviewer is one who
    A. is adept at manipulating people and circumstances toward his objective
    B. is able to put himself in the position of the interviewee
    C. gets the more difficult questions out of the way at the beginning of the interview
    D. develops one style and technique that can be used in any type of interview

3. A good interviewer guards against the tendency to form an overall opinion about an interviewee on the basis of a single aspect of the interviewee's makeup.
    This statement refers to a well-known source of error in interviewing known as the
    A. assumption error   B. expectancy error
    C. extension effect   D. halo effect

4. In conducting an "exit interview" with an employee who is leaving voluntarily, the interview's MAIN objective should be to
    A. see that the employee leaves with a good opinion of the organization
    B. learn the true reasons for the employee's resignation
    C. find out if the employee would consider a transfer
    D. try to get the employee to remain on the job

5. During an interview, an interviewee unexpectedly discloses a relevant but embarrassing personal fact.
    It would be BEST for the interviewer to
    A. listen calmly, avoiding any gesture or facial expression that would suggest approval or disapproval of what is related
    B. change the subject, since further discussion in this area may reveal other embarrassing, but irrelevant, personal facts

C. apologize to the interviewee for having led him to reveal such a fact and promise not to do so again
D. bring the interview to a close as quickly as possible in order to avoid a discussion which may be distressing to the interviewee

6. Suppose that, while you are interviewing an applicant for a position in your office, you notice a contradiction in facts in two of his responses.
For you to call the contradictions to his attention would be
    A. *inadvisable*, because it reduces the interviewee's level of participation
    B. *advisable*, because getting the facts is essential to a successful interview
    C. *inadvisable*, because the interviewer should use more subtle techniques to resolve any discrepancies
    D. *advisable*, because the interviewee should be impressed with the necessity for giving consistent answers

6.____

7. An interviewer should be aware that an undesirable result of including "leading questions" in an interview is to
    A. cause the interviewee to give a "yes" or "no" answers with qualification or explanation
    B. encourage the interviewee to discuss irrelevant topics
    C. encourage the interviewee to give more meaningful information
    D. reduce the validity of the information obtained from the interviewee

7.____

8. The kind of interview which is particularly helpful in getting an employee to tell about his complaints and grievances is one in which
    A. a pattern has been worked out involving a sequence of exact questions to be asked
    B. the interviewee is expected to support his statements with specific evidence
    C. the interviewee is not made to answer specific questions but is encouraged to talk freely
    D. the interviewer has specific items on which he wishes to get or give information

8.____

9. Suppose you are scheduled to interview an employee under your supervision concerning a health problem. You know that some of the questions you will be asking him will seem embarrassing to him, and that he may resist answering these questions.
In general, to hold these questions for the last part of the interview would be
    A. *desirable*; the intervening time period gives the interviewer an opportunity to plan how to ask these sensitive questions.
    B. *undesirable*; the employee will probably feel that he has been tricked when he suddenly must answer embarrassing questions
    C. *desirable*; the employee will probably have increased confidence in the interviewer and be more willing to answer these questions
    D. *undesirable*; questions that are important should not be deferred until the end of the interview

9.____

10. In conducting an interview, the BEST types of questions with which to begin the interview are those which the person interviewed is
    A. willing and able to answer
    B. willing but unable to answer
    C. able but unwilling to answer
    D. unable and unwilling to answer

10.____

11. In order to determine accurately a child's age, it is BEST for an interviewer to rely on
    A. the child's grade in school
    B. what the mother says
    C. birth records
    D. a library card

11.____

12. In his first interview with a new employee, it would be LEAST appropriate for a unit supervisor to
    A. find out the employee's preference for the several types of jobs to which he is able to assign him
    B. determine whether the employee will make good promotion material
    C. inform the employee of what his basic job responsibilities will be
    D. inquire about the employee's education and previous employment

12.____

13. If an interviewer takes care to phrase his questions carefully and precisely, the result will MOST probably be that
    A. he will be able to determine whether the person interviewed is being truthful
    B. the free flow of the interview will be lost
    C. he will get the information he wants
    D. he will ask stereotyped questions and narrow the scope of the interview

13.____

14. When, during an interview, is the person interviewed LEAST likely to be cautious about what he tells the interviewer?
    A. Shortly after the beginning when the questions normally suggest pleasant associations to the person interviewed
    B. As long as the interviewer keeps his questions to the point
    C. At the point where the person interviewed gains a clear insight into the area being discussed
    D. When the interview appears formally ended and goodbyes are being said

14.____

15. In an interview held for the purpose of getting information from the person interviewed, it is sometimes desirable for the interviewer to repeat the answer he has received to a question.
    For the interviewer to rephrase such an answer in his own words is good practice MAINLY because it
    A. gives the interviewer time to make up his next question
    B. gives the person interviewed a chance to correct any possible misunderstanding
    C. gives the person interviewed the feeling that the interviewer considers his answer important
    D. prevents the person interviewed from changing his answer

15.____

16. There are several methods of formulating questions during an interview. The particular method used should be adapted to the interview problems presented by the person being questioned.
Of the following methods of formulating questions during an interview, the ACCEPTABLE one is for the interviewer to ask questions which
    A. incorporate several items in order to allow a cooperative interviewee freedom to organize his statements
    B. are ambiguous in order to foil a distrustful interviewee
    C. suggest the correct answer in order to assist an interviewee who appears confused
    D. would help an otherwise unresponsive interviewee to become more responsive

16._____

17. For an interviewer to permit the person being interviewed to read the data the interviewer writes as he records the person's responses on a routine departmental form is
    A. *desirable*, because it serves to assure the person interviewed that his responses are being recorded accurately
    B. *undesirable*, because it prevents the interviewer from clarifying uncertain points by asking additional questions
    C. *desirable*, because it makes the time that the person interviewed must wait while the answer is written seem shorter
    D. *undesirable*, because it destroys the confidentiality of the interview

17._____

18. Of the following methods of conducting an interview, the BEST is to
    A. ask questions with "yes" or "no" answers
    B. listen carefully and ask only questions that are pertinent
    C. fire questions at the interviewee so that he must answer sincerely and briefly
    D. read standardized questions to the person being interviewed

18._____

KEY (CORRECT ANSWERS)

1.	A		11.	C
2.	B		12.	B
3.	D		13.	C
4.	B		14.	D
5.	A		15.	B
6.	B		16.	D
7.	D		17.	A
8.	C		18.	B
9.	C			
10.	A			

EVALUATING INFORMATION AND EVIDENCE
SAMPLE QUESTIONS

These questions test for the ability to evaluate and draw conclusions from information and evidence. Each question consists of a set of facts and a conclusion based on the facts. You must decide if the conclusion is warranted by the facts.

TEST TASK: You will be given a set of FACTS and a CONCLUSION based on the facts. The conclusion is derived from these facts only—NOT on what you may happen to know about the subject discussed. Each question has three possible answers. You must then select the correct answer in the following manner:

    Select A if the statements prove that the conclusion is TRUE.
    Select B if the statements prove that the conclusion is FALSE.
    Select C if the statements are INADEQUATE to prove the conclusion EITHER TRUE OR FALSE.

SAMPLE QUESTION #1

FACTS: All uniforms are cleaned by the Conroy Company. Blue uniforms are cleaned on Mondays or Fridays; green or brown uniforms are cleaned on Wednesdays. Alan and Jean have blue uniforms, Gary has green uniforms, and Ryan has brown uniforms.

CONCLUSION: Jean's uniforms are cleaned on Wednesdays.
The correct answer to this sample question is B.

SOLUTION: The last sentence of the FACTS says that Jean has blue uniforms. The second sentence of the FACTS says that blue uniforms are cleaned on Monday or Friday. The CONCLUSION says Jean's uniforms are cleaned on Wednesday. Wednesday is neither Monday nor Friday. Therefore, the conclusion must be FALSE (choice B).

SAMPLE QUESTION #2

FACTS: If Beth works overtime, the assignment will be completed. If the assignment is completed, then all unit employees will receive a bonus. Beth works overtime.

CONCLUSION: A bonus will be given to all employees in the unit.
The correct answer to this sample question is A.

SOLUTION: The CONCLUSION follows necessarily from the FACTS. Beth works overtime. The assignment is completed. Therefore, all unit employees will receive a bonus.

SAMPLE QUESTION #3

FACTS: Bill is older than Wanda. Edna is older than Bill. Sarah is twice as old as Wanda.

CONCLUSION: Sarah is older than Edna.
The correct answer to this Sample Question #3 is C.

SOLUTION: We know from the facts that both Sarah and Edna are older than Wanda. We do not have any other information about Sarah and Edna. Therefore, no conclusion about whether or not Sarah is older than Edna can be made.

EVALUATING INFORMATION AND EVIDENCE
EXAMINATION SECTION
TEST 1

DIRECTIONS: Each question or incomplete statement is followed by several suggested answers or completions. Select the one that BEST answers the question or completes the statement. *PRINT THE LETTER OF THE CORRECT ANSWER IN THE SPACE AT THE RIGHT.*

Questions 1-9.

DIRECTIONS: Questions 1 through 9 measure your ability to (1) determine whether statements from witnesses say essentially the same thing and (2) determine the evidence needed to make it reasonably certain that a particular conclusion is true.

1. Which of the following pairs of statements say essentially the same thing in two different ways?
    I. If you get your feet wet, you will catch a cold.
       If you catch a cold, you must have gotten your feet wet.
    II. If I am nominated, I will run for office.
       I will run for office only if I am nominated.
    The CORRECT answer is:
    A. I only   B. I and II   C. II only   D. Neither I nor II

    1.____

2. Which of the following pairs of statements say essentially the same thing in two different ways?
    I. The enzyme Rhopsin cannot be present if the bacterium Trilox is absent.
       Rhopsin and Trilox always appear together.
    II. A member of PENSA has an IQ of at least 175.
       A person with an IQ of less than 175 is not a member of PENSA
    The CORRECT answer is;
    A. I only   B. I and II   C. II only   D. Neither I nor II

    2.____

3. Which of the following pairs of statements say essentially the same thing in two different ways?
    I. None of Finer High School's sophomores will be going to the prom.
       No student at Finer High School who is going to the prom is a sophomore.
    II. If you have 20/20 vision, you may carry a firearm.
       You may not carry a firearm unless you have 20/20 vision.
    The CORRECT answer is:
    A. I only   B. I and II   C. II only   D. Neither I nor II

    3.____

4. Which of the following pairs of statements say essentially the same thing in two different ways?
   I. If the family doesn't pay the ransom, they will never see their son again.
      It is necessary for the family to pay the ransom in order for them to see their son again.
   II. If it is raining, I am carrying an umbrella.
      If I am carrying an umbrella, it is raining.
   The CORRECT answer is:
   A. I only   B. I and II   C. II only   D. Neither I nor II

5. Summary of Evidence Collected to Date:
   In the county's maternity wards, over the past year, only one baby was born who did not share a birthday with any other baby.
   Prematurely Drawn Conclusion: At least one baby was born on the same day as another baby in the county's maternity wards.
   Which of the following pieces of evidence, if any, would make it reasonably certain that the conclusion drawn is true?
   A. More than 365 babies were born in the county's maternity wards over the past year.
   B. No pairs of twins were born over the past year in the county's maternity wards.
   C. More than one baby was born in the county's maternity wards over the past year.
   D. None of the above

6. Summary of Evidence Collected to Date:
   Every claims adjustor for MetroLife drives only a Ford sedan when on the job.
   Prematurely Drawn Conclusion: A person who works for MetroLife and drives a Ford sedan is a claims adjustor.
   Which of the following pieces of evidence, if any, would make it reasonably certain that the conclusion drawn is true?
   A. Most people who work for MetroLife are claims adjustors.
   B. Some people who work for MetroLife are not claims adjustors.
   C. Most people who work for MetroLife drive Ford sedans
   D. None of the above

7. Summary of Evidence Collected to Date:
   Mason will speak to Zisk if Zisk will speak to Ronaldson.
   Prematurely Drawn Conclusion: Jones will not speak to Zisk if Zisk will speak to Ronaldson.
   Which of the following pieces of evidence, if any, would make it reasonably certain that the conclusion drawn is true?
   A. If Zisk will speak to Mason, then Ronaldson will not speak to Jones.
   B. If Mason will speak to Zisk, then Jones will not speak to Zisk.
   C. If Ronaldson will speak to Jones, then Jones will speak to Ronaldson.
   D. None of the above

8. <u>Summary of Evidence Collected to Date</u>:
No blue lights on the machine are indicators for the belt drive status.
<u>Prematurely Drawn Conclusion</u>: Some of the lights on the lower panel are not indicators for the belt drive status.
Which of the following pieces of evidence, if any, would make it reasonably certain that the conclusion drawn is true?
   A. No lights on the machine's lower panel are blue.
   B. An indicator light for the machine's belt drive status is either green or red.
   C. Some lights on the machine's lower panel are blue.
   D. None of the above

8.____

9. <u>Summary of Evidence Collected to Date</u>:
Of the four Sweeney sisters, two are married, three have brown eyes, and three are doctors.
<u>Prematurely Drawn Conclusion</u>: Two of the Sweeney sisters are brown-eyed, married doctors.
Which of the following pieces of evidence, if any, would make it reasonably certain that the conclusion is true?
   A. The sister who does not have brown eyes is married.
   B. The sister who does not have brown eyes is not a doctor, and one who is not married is not a doctor.
   C. Every Sweeney sister with brown eyes is a doctor.
   D. None of the above

9.____

Questions 10-14.

DIRECTIONS: Questions 10 through 14 refer to Map #5 and measure your ability to orient yourself within a given section of town, neighborhood or particular area. Each of the questions describes a starting point and a destination. Assume that you are driving a car in the area shown on the map accompanying the questions. Use the map as a basis for the shortest way to get from one point to another without breaking the law.

On the map, a street marked by arrows, or by arrows and the words "One Way," indicates one-way travel and should be assumed to be one-way for the entire length, even when there are breaks or jogs in the street. EXCEPTION: A street that does not have the same name over the full length.

4 (#1)

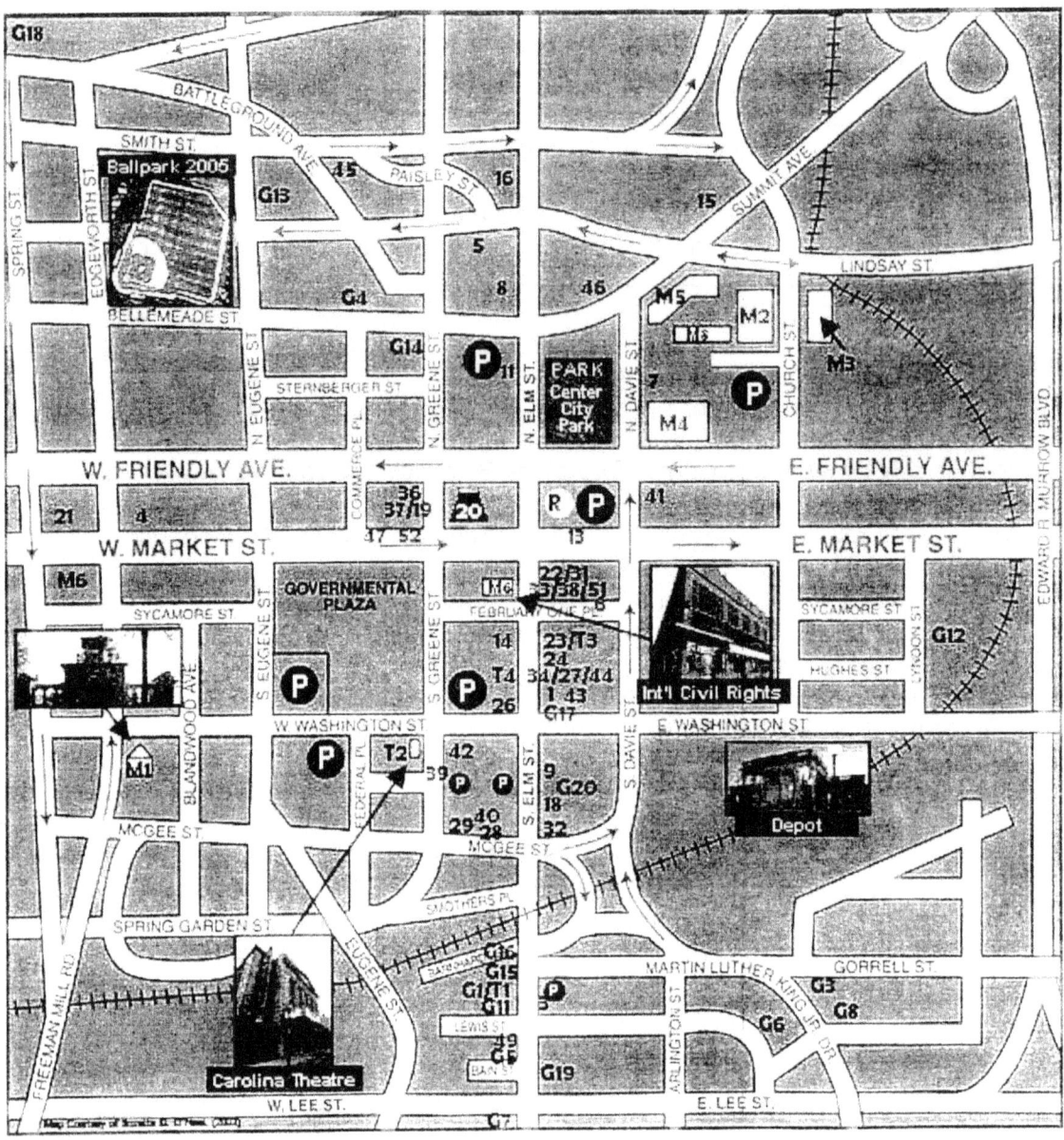

Map #5

10. The SHORTEST legal way from the depot to Center City Park is 10.____
    A. north on Church, west on Market, north on Elm
    B. east on Washington, north on Edward R. Murrow Blvd., west on Friendly Ave.
    C. west on Washington, north on Greene, east on Market, north on Davie
    D. north on Church, west on Friendly Ave.

11. The SHORTEST legal way from the Governmental Plaza to the Ballpark is 11._____
    A. west on Market, north on Edgeworth
    B. west on Market, north on Eugene
    C. north on Greene, west on Lindsay
    D. north on Commerce Place, west on Bellemeade

12. The SHORTEST legal way from the International Civil Rights Building to the building marked "M3" on the map is 12._____
    A. east on February One Place, north on Davie, east on Friendly Ave., north on Church
    B. south on Elm, west on Washington, north on Greene, east on Market, north on Church
    C. north on Elm, east on Market, north on Church
    D. north on Elm, east on Lindsay, south on Church

13. The SHORTEST legal way from the Ballpark to the Carolina Theatre is 13._____
    A. east on Lindsay, south on Greene
    B. south on Edgeworth, east on Friendly Ave., south on Greene
    C. east on Bellemeade, south on Elm, west on Washington

14. A car traveling north or south on Church Street may NOT go 14._____
    A. west onto Friendly Ave.   B. west onto Lindsay
    C. east onto Market   D. west onto Smith

Questions 15-19.

DIRECTIONS: Questions 15 through 19 refer to Figure #3, on the following page, and measure your ability to understand written descriptions of events. Each question presents a description of an accident or event and asks you which of the following five drawings in Figure #3 BEST represents it.
In the drawings, the following symbols are used:
Moving vehicle ◊   Non-moving vehicle ♦
Pedestrian or bicyclist •
The path and direction of travel of a vehicle or pedestrian is indicated by a solid line.
The path and direction of travel of each vehicle or pedestrian directly involved in a collision from the point of impact is indicated by a dotted line.

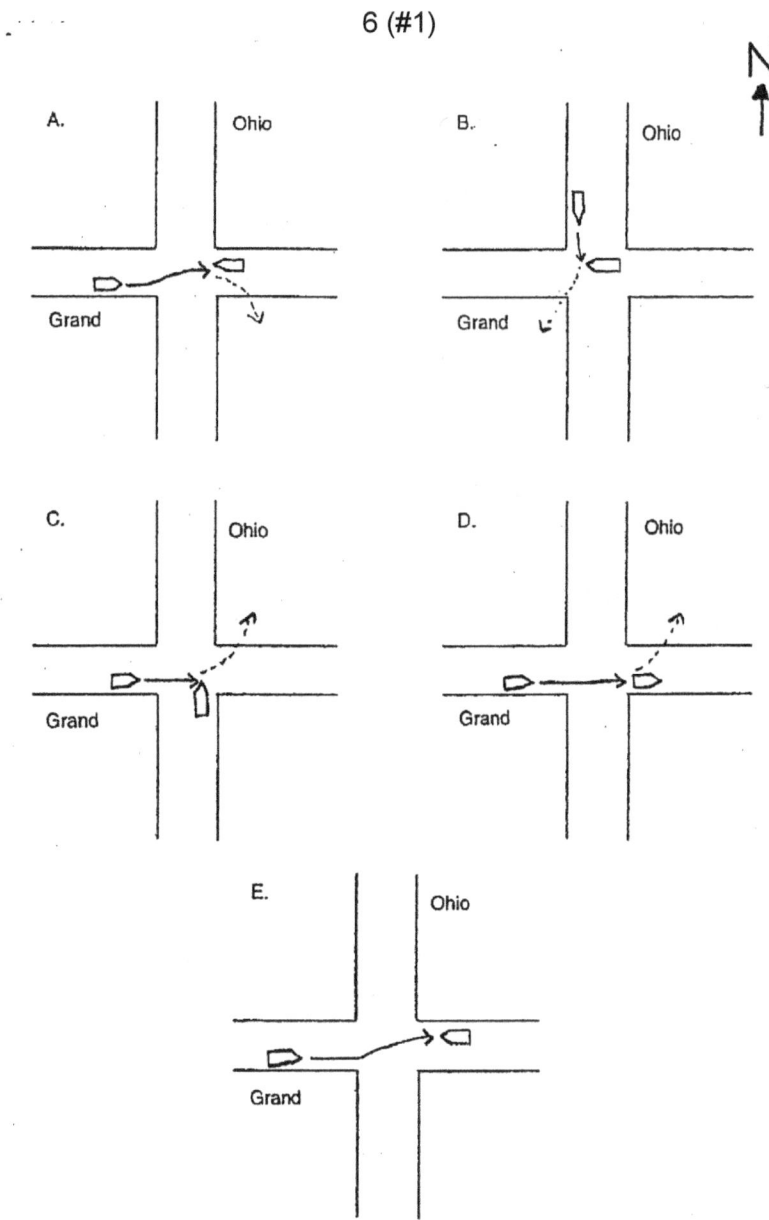

In the space at the right, print the letter of the drawing that BEST fit the descriptions written below.

15. A driver headed south on Ohio runs a red light and strikes the front of a car headed west on Grand. He glances off and leaves the roadway at the southwest corner of Grand and Ohio.   15._____

16. A driver heading east on Grand drifts into the oncoming lane as it travels through the intersection of Grand and Ohio, and strikes an oncoming car head-on   16._____

17. A driver heading east on Grand veers into the oncoming lane, sideswipes a westbound car and overcorrects as he swerves back into his lane. He leaves the roadway near the southeast corner of Grand and Ohio.

17._____

18. A driver heading east on Grand strikes the front of a car that is traveling north on Ohio and has run a red light. After striking the front of the northbound car, the driver veers left and leaves the roadway at the northeast corner of Grand and Ohio.

18._____

19. A driver heading east on Grand is traveling above the speed limit and clips the rear end of another eastbound car. The driver then veers to the left and leaves the roadway at the northeast corner of Grand and Ohio.

19._____

Questions 20-22.

DIRECTIONS: In Questions 20 through 22, choose the word or phrase CLOSEST in meaning to the word or phrase printed in capital letters.

20. PETITION
    A. appeal   B. law   C. oath   D. opposition

20._____

21. MALPRACTICE
    A. commission   B. mayhem   C. error   D. misconduct

21._____

22. EXONERATE
    A. incriminate   B. accuse   C. lengthen   D. acquit

22._____

Questions 23-25.

DIRECTIONS: Questions 23 through 25 measure your ability to do fieldwork-related arithmetic. Each question presents a separate arithmetic problem for you to solve.

23. Officers Lane and Bryant visited another city as part of an investigation. Because each is from a different precinct, they agree to split all expenses. With her credit card, Lane paid $70 for food and $150 for lodging. Bryant wrote checks for gas ($50) and entertainment ($40).
How much does Bryant owe Lane?
    A. $65   B. $90   C. $155   D. $210

23._____

24. In a remote mountain pass, two search-and-rescue teams, one from Silverton and one from Durango, combine to look for a family that disappeared in a recent snowstorm. The combined team is composed of 20 members.
Which of the following statements could NOT be true?
    A. The Durango team has a dozen members.
    B. The Silverton team has only one member.
    C. The Durango team has two more members than the Silverton team.
    D. The Silverton team has one more member than the Durango team.

24._____

25. Three people in the department share a vehicle for a period of one year. The average number of miles traveled per month by each person is 150.
How many miles will be added to the car's odometer at the end of the year?
A. 1,800 B. 2,400 C. 3,600 D. 5,400

25._____

KEY (CORRECT ANSWERS)

1. D
2. C
3. A
4. A
5. A

6. A
7. B
8. C
9. B
10. D

11. D
12. C
13. D
14. D
15. B

16. E
17. A
18. C
19. D
20. A

21. D
22. D
23. A
24. D
25. D

SOLUTIONS TO QUESTIONS 1-9

P implies Q = original statement

Not Q implies not P = contrapositive of the original statement. A statement and its contrapositive are logically equivalent.

Q implies P = converse of the original statement

Not P implies not Q = inverse of the original statement. The converse and inverse of an original statement are logically equivalent.

P implies Q = Not P or Q.

1. The CORRECT answer is D.
   In items I and II, each statement is the converses of the other. A converse of a statement is not equivalent to its original statement.

2. The CORRECT answer is C.
   In item I, the first statement is equivalent to "If Trilox is absent, then Rhopsin is also absent." But this does NOT imply that if Trilox is present, so too must Rhopsin be present. In item II, each statement is the contrapositive of the other. Thus, they are equivalent.

3. The CORRECT answer is A.
   In item I, the first sentence tells us that if a student is a sophomore, he/she will not go the prom. The second statement is equivalent to "If a student does attend the prom, he/she is not a sophomore." This is the contrapositive of the first statement, (so it is equivalent to it).

4. The CORRECT answer is A.
   In item I, the second statement can be written as "If the family sees their son again, then they must have paid the ransom." This is the contrapositive of the first statement. In item II, these statements are converses of each other; thus, they are not equivalent.

5. The CORRECT answer is A.
   If more than 365 babies were born in the county in one year, then at least two babies must share the same birthday.

6. The CORRECT answer is A.
   Given that most people who work for MetroLife are claims adjustors, plus the fact that all claims adjustors drive only a Ford sedan, it is a reasonable conclusion that any person who drives a Ford sedan and works for MetroLife is a claims adjustor.

7. The CORRECT answer is B.
   Jones will not speak to Zisk if Zisk will speak to Ronaldson, which will happen if Mason will speak to Zisk.

8. The CORRECT answer is C.
We are given that blue lights are never an indicator for the drive belt status. If some of the lights on the lower panel of the machine are blue, then it is reasonable to conclude that some of the lights on the lower panel are not indicators for the drive belt status.

9. The CORRECT answer is B.
There is only one sister that does not have brown eyes and only one sister that is not a doctor, and if the information in answer B is correct, then we learn that the same sister is a non-doctor without brown eyes. We also learn that this same non-doctor is not married. Since this all describes the same sister, we can conclude that two of the other sisters must be married doctors with brown eyes.

TEST 2

DIRECTIONS: Each question or incomplete statement is followed by several suggested answers or completions. Select the one that BEST answers the question or completes the statement. *PRINT THE LETTER OF THE CORRECT ANSWER IN THE SPACE AT THE RIGHT.*

Questions 1-9.

DIRECTIONS: Questions 1 through 9 measure your ability to (1) determine whether statements from witnesses say essentially the same thing and (2) determine the evidence needed to make it reasonably certain that a particular conclusion is true.
To do well on this part of the test, you do NOT have to have a working knowledge of police procedures and techniques. Nor do you have to have any more familiarity with criminals and criminal behavior than that acquired from reading newspapers, listening to radio or watching TV. To do well in this part, you must read and reason carefully.

1. Which of the following pairs of statements say essentially the same thing in two different ways? 1.____
    I. If there is life on Mars, we should fund NASA.
       Either there is life on Mars, or we should not fund NASA.
    II. All Eagle Scouts are teenage boys.
        All teenage boy are Eagle Scouts.
    The CORRECT answer is:
       A. I only   B. I and II   C. II only   D. Neither I nor II

2. Which of the following pairs of statements say essentially the same thing in two different ways? 2.____
    I. If that notebook is missing its front cover, it definitely belongs to Carter.
       Carter's notebook is the only one missing its front cover.
    II. If it's hot, the pool is open.
        The pool is open if it's hot.
    The CORRECT answer is:
       A. I only   B. I and II   C. II only   D. Neither I nor II

3. Which of the following pairs of statements say essentially the same thing in two different ways? 3.____
    I. Nobody who works at the mill is without benefits.
       Everyone who works at the mill has benefits.
    II. We will fund the program only if at least 100 people sign the petition.
        Either we will fund the program or at least 100 people will sign the petition.
    The CORRECT answer is:
       A. I only   B. I and II   C. II only   D. Neither I nor II

4. Which of the following pairs of statements say essentially the same thing in two different ways?
   I. If the new parts arrive, Mr. Luther's request has been answered.
      Mr. Luther requested new parts to arrive.
   II. The machine's test cycle will not run unless the operation cycle is not running.
      The machine's test cycle must be running in order for the operation cycle to run.
   The CORRECT answer is:
   A. I only   B. I and II   C. II only   D. Neither I nor II

5. Summary of Evidence Collected to Date:
   I. To become a member of the East Side Crips, a kid must be either "jumped in" or steal a squad car without getting caught.
   II. Sid, a kid on the East Side, was caught stealing a squad car.
   Prematurely Drawn Conclusion: Sid did not become a member of the East Side Crips.
   Which of the following pieces of evidence, if any, would make it reasonably certain that the conclusion drawn is true?
   A. "Jumping in" is not allowed in prison.
   B. Sid was not "jumped in."
   C. Sid's stealing the squad car had nothing to do with wanting to join the East Side Crips.
   D. None of the above

6. Summary of Evidence Collected to Date:
   I. Jones, a Precinct 8 officer, has more arrests than Smith.
   II. Smith and Watson have exactly the same number of arrests.
   Prematurely Drawn Conclusion: Watson is not a Precinct 8 officer.
   Which of the following pieces of evidence, if any, would make it reasonably certain that the conclusion drawn is true?
   A. All the officers in Precinct 8 have more arrests than Watson.
   B. All the officers in Precinct 8 have fewer arrests than Watson.
   C. Watson has fewer arrests than Jones.
   D. None of the above

7. Summary of Evidence Collected to Date:
   I. Twenty one-dollar bills are divided among Frances, Kerry, and Brian.
   II. If Kerry gives her dollar bills to Frances, then Frances will have more money than Brian.
   Prematurely Drawn Conclusion: Frances has twelve dollars.
   Which of the following pieces of evidence, if any, would make it reasonably certain that the conclusion drawn is true?
   A. If Brian gives his dollars to Kerry, then Kerry will have more money than Frances.
   B. Brian has two dollars.
   C. If Kerry gives her dollars to Brian, Brian will still have less money than Frances.
   D. None of the above

8. Summary of Evidence Collected to Date:
   I. The street sweepers will be here at noon today.
   II. Residents on the west side of the street should move their cars before noon.
   Prematurely Drawn Conclusion: Today is Wednesday.
   Which of the following pieces of evidence, if any, would make it reasonably certain that the conclusion drawn is true?
   A. The street sweepers never sweep the east side of the street on Wednesday.
   B. The street sweepers arrive at noon every other day.
   C. There is no parking allowed on the west side of the street on Wednesday.
   D. None of the above

8._____

9. Summary of Evidence Collected to Date:
   The only time the warning light comes on is when there is a power surge.
   Prematurely Drawn Conclusion: The warning light does not come on if the air conditioner is not running.
   Which of the following pieces of evidence, if any, would make it reasonably certain that the conclusion drawn is true?
   A. The air conditioner does not turn on if the warning light is on.
   B. Sometimes a power surge is caused by the dishwasher.
   C. There is only a power surge when the air conditioner turns on.
   D. None of the above

9._____

Questions 10-14.

DIRECTIONS: Questions 10 through 14 refer to Map #3 and measure your ability to orient yourself within a given section of town, neighborhood or particular area. Each of the questions describes a starting point and a destination. Assume that you are driving a car in the area shown on the map accompanying the questions. Use the map as a basis for the shortest way to get from one point to another without breaking the law.
On the map, a street marked by arrows, or by arrows and the words "One Way," indicates one-way travel and should be assumed to be one-way for the entire length, even when there are breaks or jogs in the street. EXCEPTION: A street that does not have the same name over the full length.

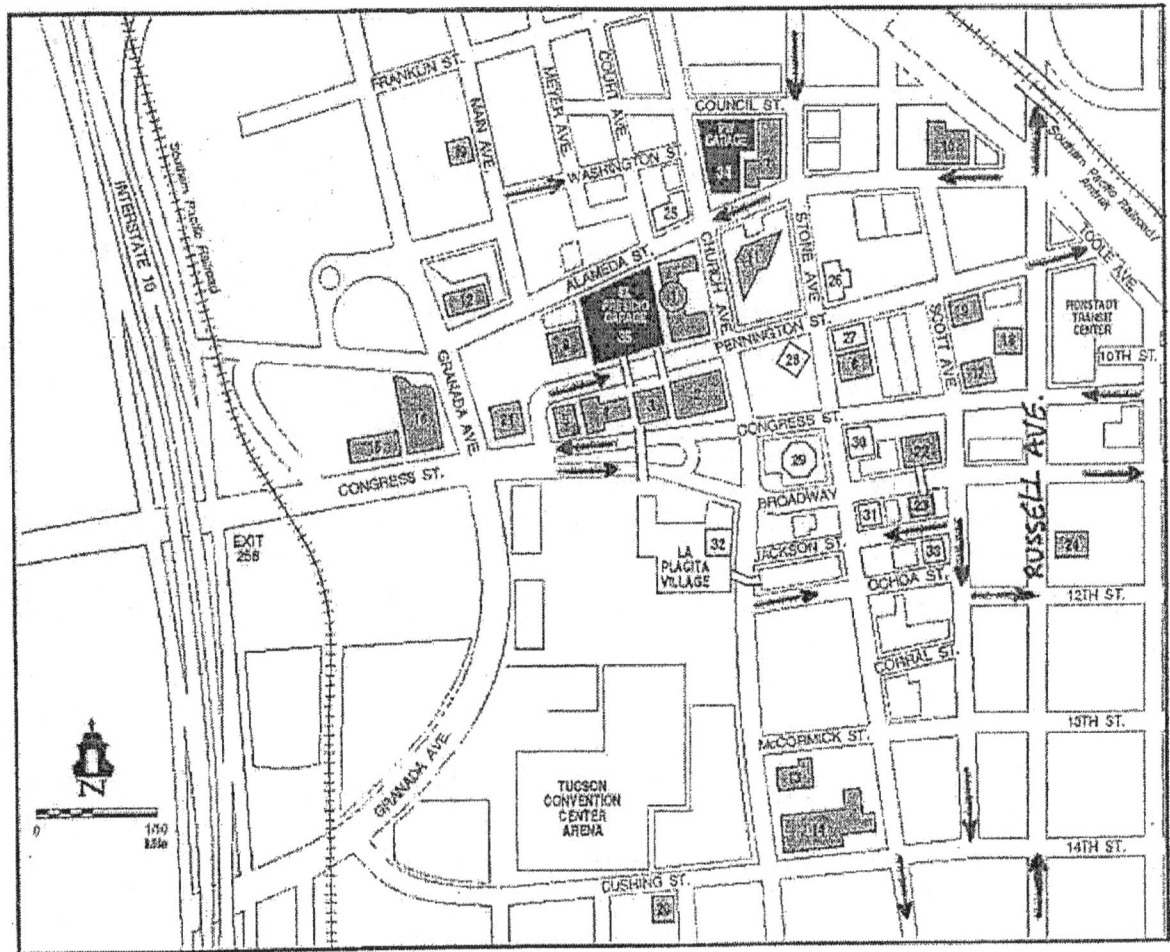

PIMA COUNTY
1. Old Courthouse
2. Superior Court Building
3. Administration Building
4. Health and Welfare Building
5. Mechanical Building
6. Legal Services Building
7. County/City Public Works Center

CITY OF TUCSON
8. City Hall
9. City Hall Annex
10. Alameda Plaza City Court Building
11. Public Library – Main Branch
12. Tucson Water Building
13. Fire Department Headquarters
14. Police Department Building

10. The SHORTEST legal way from the Public Library to the Alameda Plaza City Court Building is
   A. north on Stone Ave., east of Alameda
   B. south on Stone Ave., east on Congress, north on Russell Ave., west on Alameda
   C. south on Stone Ave., east on Pennington, north on Russell Ave., west on Alameda
   D. south on Church Ave., east on Pennington, north on Russell Ave., west on Alameda

5 (#2)

11. The SHORTEST legal way from City Hall to the Police Department is　　　　11._____
    A. east on Congress, south on Scott Ave., west on 14th
    B. east on Pennington, south on Stone Ave.
    C. east on Congress, south on Stone Ave.
    D. east on Pennington, south on Church Ave.

12. The SHORTEST legal way from the Tucson Water Building to the Legal Service　　12._____
    Building is
    A. south on Granada Ave., east on Congress, north to east on Pennington, south on Stone Ave.
    B. east on Alameda, south on Church Ave., east on Pennington, south on Stone Ave.
    C. north on Granada Ave., east on Washington, south on Church Ave., east on Pennington, south on Stone Ave.
    D. south on Granada Ave., east on Cushing, north on Stone Ave.

13. The SHORTEST legal way from the Tucson Convention Center Arena to the　　13._____
    City Hall Annex is
    A. west on Cushing, north on Granada Ave., east on Congress east on Broadway
    B. east on Cushing, north on Church Ave., east on Pennington
    C. east on Cushing, north on Russel Ave., west on Pennington
    D. east on Cushing, north on Stone Ave., east on Pennington

14. The SHORTEST legal way from Ronstadt Transit Center to the Fire Department　　14._____
    is
    A. west on Pennington, south on Stone Ave., west on McCormick
    B. west on Congress, south on Russell Ave., west on 13th
    C. west on Congress, south on Church Ave.
    D. west on Pennington, south on Church Ave.

Questions 15-19.

DIRECTIONS:　Questions 15 through 19 refer to Figure #3, on the following page, and measure your ability to understand written descriptions of events. Each question presents a description of an accident or event and asks you which of the following five drawings in Figure #3 BEST represents it.
In the drawings, the following symbols are used:
Moving vehicle ◊　　　　Non-moving vehicle ▮
Pedestrian or bicyclist •
The path and direction of travel of a vehicle or pedestrian is indicated by a solid line.
The path and direction of travel of each vehicle or pedestrian directly involved in a collision from the point of impact is indicated by a dotted line.

In the space at the right, print the letter of the drawing that BEST fit the descriptions written below.

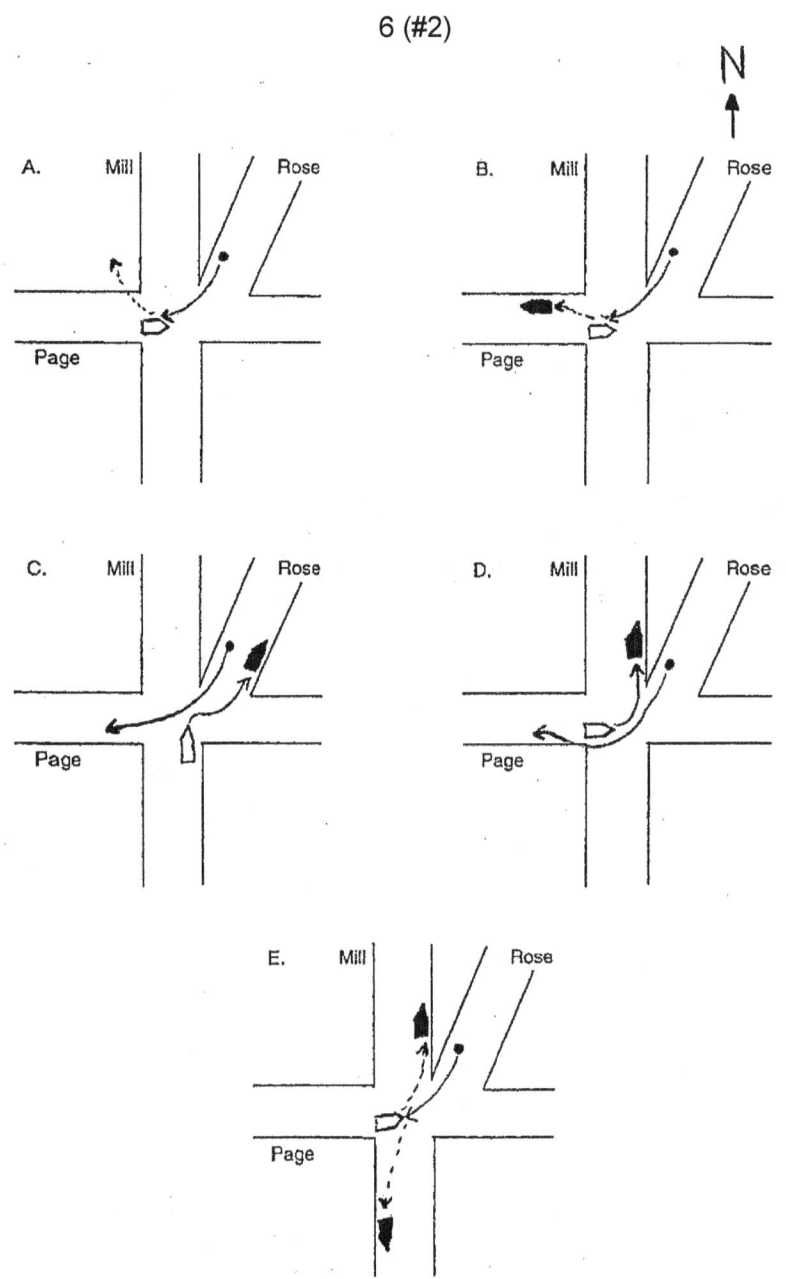

15. A bicyclist heading southwest on Rose travels into the intersection, sideswipes a car that is heading east on Page, and veers right, leaving the roadway at the northwest corner of Page and Mill.

15.____

16. A driver traveling north on Mill swerves right to avoid a bicyclist that is traveling southwest on Rose. The driver strikes the rear end of a car parked on Rose. The bicyclist continues through the intersection and travels west on Page.

16.____

17. A bicyclist heading southwest on Rose travels into the intersection, sideswipes a car that is heading east on Page, and veers right, striking the rear end of a car parked in the westbound lane on Page.

17.____

18. A driver traveling east on Page swerves left to avoid a bicyclist that is traveling southwest on Rose. The driver strikes the rear end of a car parked on Mill. The bicyclist continues through the intersection and travels west on Page.

18._____

19. A bicyclist heading southwest on Rose enters the intersection and sideswipes a car that is swerving left to avoid her. The bicyclist veers left and collides with a car parked in the southbound lane on Mill. The driver of the car veers left and collides with a car parked in the northbound lane on Mill.

19._____

Questions 20-22.

DIRECTIONS: In Questions 20 through 22, choose the word or phrase CLOSEST in meaning to the word or phrase printed in capital letters.

20. WAIVE
    A. cease   B. surrender   C. prevent   D. die

20._____

21. DEPOSITION
    A. settlement   B. deterioration   C. testimony   D. character

21._____

22. IMMUNITY
    A. exposure   B. accusation   C. protection   D. exchange

22._____

Questions 23-25.

DIRECTIONS: Questions 23 through 25 measure your ability to do fieldwork-related arithmetic. Each question presents a separate arithmetic problem for you to solve.

23. Dean, a claims investigator, is reading a 445-page case record in his spare time at work. He has already read 157 pages.
If Dean reads 24 pages a day, he should finish reading the rest of the record in _____ days.
    A. 7   B. 12   C. 19   D. 24

23._____

24. The Fire Department owns four cars. The Department of Sanitation owns twice as many cars as the Fire Department. The Department of Parks and Recreation owns one fewer car than the Department of Sanitation. The Department of Parks and Recreation is buying new tires for each of its cars. Each tire costs $100.
How much is the Department of Parks and Recreation going to spend on tires?
    A. $400   B. $2,800   C. $3,200   D. $4,900

24._____

25. A dance hall is about 5,000 square feet. The local ordinance does not allow more than 50 people per every 100 square feet of commercial space.
The maximum capacity of the hall is
    A. 500   B. 2,500   C. 5,000   D. 25,000

25._____

KEY (CORRECT ANSWERS)

1.	D	11.	D
2.	B	12.	A
3.	A	13.	B
4.	D	14.	C
5.	B	15.	A
6.	D	16.	C
7.	D	17.	B
8.	A	18.	D
9.	C	19.	E
10.	C	20.	B

21. C
22. C
23. B
24. B
25. B

SOLUTIONS TO QUESTIONS 1-9

P implies Q = original statement

Not Q implies not P = contrapositive of the original statement. A statement and its contrapositive are logically equivalent.

Q implies P = converse of the original statement

Not P implies not Q = inverse of the original statement. The converse and inverse of an original statement are logically equivalent.

P implies Q = Not P or Q.

1. The CORRECT answer is D.
   For item I, the second statement should be "Either there is no life on Mars or we should fund NASA" in order to be logically equivalent to the first statement. For item II, the statements are converses of each other; thus, they are not equivalent.

2. The CORRECT answer is B.
   In item I, this is an example of P implies Q and Q implies P. In this case, P = the notebook is missing its cover and Q = the notebook belongs to Carter. In item II, the ordering of the words is changed, but the If P then Q is exactly the same. P = it is hot and Q = the pool is open.

3. The CORRECT answer is A.
   For item I, if nobody is without benefits, then everybody has benefits. For item II, the second equivalent statement should be "either we will not fund the program or at least 100 people will sign the petition."

4. The CORRECT answer is D.
   For item I, the first statement is an implication, whereas the second statement mentions only one part of the implication (new parts are requested) and says nothing about the other part. For item II, the first statement is equivalent to "if the operating cycle is not running, then the test cycle will run." The second statement is equivalent to "if the operating cycle is running, then the test cycle will run." So, these statements in item II are not equivalent.

5. The CORRECT answer is B.
   Since Sid did not steal a car and avoid getting caught, the only other way he could become a Crips member would be "jumped in." Choice B tells us that Sid was not "jumped in," so we conclude that he did not become a member of the Crips.

6. The CORRECT answer is D.
   Since Smith and Watson have the same number of arrests, Watson must have fewer arrests than Jones. This means that each of choices A and B is impossible. Choice C would also not reveal whether or not Watson is a Precinct 8 officer.

7. The CORRECT answer is D.
Exact dollar amounts still cannot be ascertained by using any of the other choices.

8. The CORRECT answer is A.
The street sweepers never sweep on the east side of the street on Wednesday; however, they will be here at noon today. This implies that they will sweep on the west side of the street. Since the residents should move their cars before noon, we can conclude that today is Wednesday.

9. The CORRECT answer is C.
We start with W implies P, where W = warning light comes on and P = power surge. Choice C would read as P implies A, where A = air conditioning is running. Combining these statements leads to W implies A. The conclusion can be read as: Not A implies Not W, which is equivalent to W implies A.

EVALUATING CONCLUSIONS IN LIGHT OF KNOWN FACTS
EXAMINATION SECTION
TEST 1

DIRECTIONS: Each question or incomplete statement is followed by several suggested answers or completions. Select the one that BEST answers the question or completes the statement. *PRINT THE LETTER OF THE CORRECT ANSWER IN THE SPACE AT THE RIGHT.*

Questions 1-9.

DIRECTIONS: In Questions 1 through 9, you will read a set of facts and a conclusion drawn from them. The conclusion may be valid or invalid, based on the facts. It is your task to determine the validity of the conclusion.
For each question, select the letter before the statement that BEST expresses the relationship between the given facts and the conclusion that has been drawn from them. Your choices are:
   A. The facts prove the conclusion.
   B. The facts disprove the conclusion; or
   C. The facts neither prove nor disprove the conclusion.

1. FACTS: Lauren must use Highway 29 to get to work. Lauren has a meeting today at 9:00 A.M. If she misses the meeting, Lauren will probably lose a major account. Highway 29 is closed all day today for repairs.

    CONCLUSION: Lauren will not be able to get to work.

    A. The facts prove the conclusion.
    B. The facts disprove the conclusion.
    C. The facts neither prove nor disprove the conclusion.

1._____

2. FACTS: The Tumbleweed Follies, a traveling burlesque show, is looking for a new line dancer. The position requires both singing and dancing skills. If the show cannot fill the position by Friday, it will begin to look for a magician to fill the time slot currently held by the line dancers. Willa, who wants to audition for the line dancing position, can sing, but cannot dance.

    CONCLUSION: Willa is qualified to audition for the part of line dancer.

    A. The facts prove the conclusion.
    B. The facts disprove the conclusion.
    C. The facts neither prove nor disprove the conclusion.

2._____

2 (#1)

3. FACTS: Terry owns two dogs, Spike and Stan. One of the dogs is short-haired and has blue eyes. One dog as a pink nose. The blue-eyed dog never barks. One of the dogs has white fur on its paws. Sam has long hair.

   CONCLUSION: Spike never barks.

   A. The facts prove the conclusion.
   B. The facts disprove the conclusion.
   C. The facts neither prove nor disprove the conclusion.

3.____

4. FACTS: No science teachers are members of the PTA. Some English teachers are members of the PTA. Some English teachers in the PTA also wear glasses. Every PTA member is required to sit on the dunking stool at the student carnival except for those who wear glasses, who will be exempt. Those who are exempt, however, will have to officiate the hamster races. All of the English teachers in the PTA who do not wear glasses are married.

   CONCLUSION: All the married English teachers in the PTA will set on the dunking stool at the student carnival.

   A. The facts prove the conclusion.
   B. The facts disprove the conclusion.
   C. The facts neither prove nor disprove the conclusion.

4.____

5. FACTS: If the price of fuel is increased and sales remain constant, oil company profits will increase. The price of fuel was increased, and market experts project that sales levels are likely to be maintained.

   CONCLUSION: The price of fuel will increase.

   A. The facts prove the conclusion.
   B. The facts disprove the conclusion.
   C. The facts neither prove nor disprove the conclusion.

5.____

6. FACTS: Some members of the gymnastics team are double-jointed, and some members of the gymnastics team ae also on the lacrosse team. Some double-jointed members of the gymnastics team are also coaches. All gymnastics team members perform floor exercises, except the coaches. All the double-jointed members of the gymnastics team who are not coaches are freshmen.

   CONCLUSION: Some double-jointed freshmen are coaches.

   A. The facts prove the conclusion.
   B. The facts disprove the conclusion.
   C. The facts neither prove nor disprove the conclusion.

6.____

7. FACTS: Each member of the International Society speaks at least one foreign language, but no member speaks more than four foreign languages. Five members speak Spanish; three speak Mandarin; four speak French; four speak German; and five speak a foreign language other than Spanish, Mandarin, French, or German.

    CONCLUSION: The lowest possible number of members in the International Society is eight.

    A. The facts prove the conclusion.
    B. The facts disprove the conclusion.
    C. The facts neither prove nor disprove the conclusion.

7.____

8. FACTS: Mary keeps seven cats in her apartment. Only three of the cats will eat the same kind of food. Mary wants to keep at least one extra bag of each kind of food.

    CONCLUSION: The minimum number of bags Mary will need to keep as extra is 7.

    A. The facts prove the conclusion.
    B. The facts disprove the conclusion.
    C. The facts neither prove nor disprove the conclusion.

8.____

9. FACTS: In Ed and Marie's exercise group, everyone likes the treadmill or the stationary bicycle, or both, but Ed does not like the stationary bicycle. Marie has not expressed a preference, but spends most of her time on the stationary bicycle.

    CONCLUSION: Everyone in the group who does not like the treadmill likes the stationary bicycle.

    A. The facts prove the conclusion.
    B. The facts disprove the conclusion.
    C. The facts neither prove nor disprove the conclusion.

9.____

Questions 10-17.

DIRECTIONS: Questions 10 through 17 are based on the following reading passage. It is not your knowledge of the particular topic that is being tested, but your ability to reason based on what you have read. The passage is likely to detail several proposed courses of action and factors affecting these proposals. The reading passage is followed by a conclusion or outcome based on the facts in the passage, or a description of a decision taken regarding the situation. The conclusion is followed by a number of statements that have a possible connection to the conclusion. For each statement, you are to determine whether:

A. The statement proves the conclusion.
B. The statement supports the conclusion but does not prove it.
C. The statement disproves the conclusion.
D. The statement weakens the conclusion but does not disprove it.
E. The statement has no relevance to the conclusion.

Remember that the conclusion after the passage is to be accepted as the outcome of what actually happened, and that you are being asked to evaluate the impact each statement would have had on the conclusion.

PASSAGE

The Owyhee Mission School District's Board of Directors is hosting a public meeting to debate the merits of the proposed abolition of all bilingual education programs within the district. The group that has made the proposal believes the programs, which teach immigrant children academic subjects in their native language until they have learned English well enough to join mainstream classes, inhibit the ability of students to acquire English quickly and succeed in school and in the larger American society. Such programs, they argue, are also a wasteful drain on the district's already scant resources.

At the meeting, several teachers and parents stand to speak out against the proposal. The purpose of an education, they say, should be to build upon, rather than dismantle, a minority child's language and culture. By teaching children in academic subjects in their native tongues, while simultaneously offering English language instruction, schools can meet the goals of learning English and progressing through academic subjects along with their peers.

Hiram Nguyen, a representative of the parents whose children are currently enrolled in bilingual education, stands at the meeting to express the parents' wishes. The parents have been polled, he says, and are overwhelmingly of the opinion that while language and culture are important to them, they are not things that will disappear from the students' lives if they are no longer taught in the classroom. The most important issue for the parents is whether their children will succeed in school and be competitive in the larger American society. If bilingual education can be demonstrated to do that, then the parents are in favor of continuing it.

At the end of the meeting, a proponent of the plan, Oscar Ramos, stands to clarify some misconceptions about the proposal. It does not call for a "sink or swim" approach, he says, but allows for an interpreter to be present in mainstream classes to explain anything a student finds too complex or confusing.

The last word of the meeting is given to Delia Cruz, a bilingual teacher at one of the district's elementary schools. A student is bound to find anything complex or confusing, she says, if it is spoken in a language he has never heard before. It is more wasteful to place children in classrooms where they don't understand anything, she says, than it is to try to teach them something useful as they are learning the English language.

CONCLUSION: After the meeting, the Owyhee Mission School District's Board of Directors votes to terminate all the district's bilingual education programs at the end of the current academic year, but to maintain the current level of funding to each of the schools that have programs cut.

10. A poll conducted by the *Los Angeles Times* at approximately the same time as the Board's meeting indicated that 75% of the people were opposed to bilingual education; among Latinos, opposition was 84%.
    A. The statement proves the conclusion.
    B. The statement supports the conclusion but does not prove it.
    C. The statement disproves the conclusion.
    D. The statement weakens the conclusion but does not disprove it.
    E. The statement has no relevance to the conclusion.

11. Of all the studies connected on bilingual education programs, 64% indicate that students learned English grammar better in "sink or swim" classes without any special features than they did in bilingual education classes.
    A. The statement proves the conclusion.
    B. The statement supports the conclusion but does not prove it.
    C. The statement disproves the conclusion.
    D. The statement weakens the conclusion but does not disprove it.
    E. The statement has no relevance to the conclusion.

12. In the academic year that begins after the Board's vote, Montgomery Burns Elementary, an Owyhee Mission District school, launches a new bilingual program for the children of Somali immigrants.
    A. The statement proves the conclusion.
    B. The statement supports the conclusion but does not prove it.
    C. The statement disproves the conclusion.
    D. The statement weakens the conclusion but does not disprove it.
    E. The statement has no relevance to the conclusion.

13. In the previous academic year, under severe budget restraints, the Owyhee Mission District cut all physical education, music, and art classes, but its funding for bilingual education classes increased by 18%.
    A. The statement proves the conclusion.
    B. The statement supports the conclusion but does not prove it.
    C. The statement disproves the conclusion.
    D. The statement weakens the conclusion but does not disprove it.
    E. The statement has no relevance to the conclusion.

14. Before the Board votes, a polling consultant conducts randomly sampled assessments of immigrant students who enrolled in Owyhee District schools at a time when they did not speak any English at all. Ten years after graduating from high school, 44% of those who received bilingual education were professionals – doctors, lawyers, educators, engineers, etc. Of those who did not receive bilingual education, 38% were professionals.
    A. The statement proves the conclusion.
    B. The statement supports the conclusion but does not prove it.
    C. The statement disproves the conclusion.
    D. The statement weakens the conclusion but does not disprove it.
    E. The statement has no relevance to the conclusion.

15. Over the past several years, the scores of Owyhee District students have gradually declined, and enrollment numbers have followed as anxious parents transferred their children to other schools or applied for a state-funded voucher program.

    A. The statement proves the conclusion.
    B. The statement supports the conclusion but does not prove it.
    C. The statement disproves the conclusion.
    D. The statement weakens the conclusion but does not disprove it.
    E. The statement has no relevance to the conclusion.

    15.____

16. California and Massachusetts, two of the most liberal states in the country, have each passed ballot measures banning bilingual education in public schools.

    A. The statement proves the conclusion.
    B. The statement supports the conclusion but does not prove it.
    C. The statement disproves the conclusion.
    D. The statement weakens the conclusion but does not disprove it.
    E. The statement has no relevance to the conclusion.

    16.____

17. In the academic year that begins after the Board's vote, no Owyhee Mission Schools are conducting bilingual instruction.

    A. The statement proves the conclusion.
    B. The statement supports the conclusion but does not prove it.
    C. The statement disproves the conclusion.
    D. The statement weakens the conclusion but does not disprove it.
    E. The statement has no relevance to the conclusion.

    17.____

Questions 18-25.

DIRECTIONS: Questions 18 through 25 each provide four factual statements and a conclusion based on these statements. After reading the entire question, you will decide whether:
   A. The conclusion is proved by Statements 1-4;
   B. The conclusion is disproved by Statements 1-4;
   C. The facts are not sufficient to prove or disprove the conclusion.

18. FACTUAL STATEMENTS:
    1) Gear X rotates in a clockwise direction if Switch C is in the OFF position.
    2) Gear X will rotate in a counter-clockwise direction if Switch C is ON.
    3) If Gear X is rotating in a clockwise direction, then Gear Y will not be rotating at all.
    4) Switch C is OFF.

    CONCLUSION: Gear Y is rotating.

    A. The conclusion is proved by Statements 1-4;
    B. The conclusion is disproved by Statements 1-4;
    C. The facts are not sufficient to prove or disprove the conclusion.

    18.____

7 (#1)

19. FACTUAL STATEMENTS:
    1) Mark is older than Jim but younger than Dan.
    2) Fern is older than Mark but younger than Silas.
    3) Dan is younger than Silas but older than Edward.
    4) Edward is older than Mark but younger than Fern.

    CONCLUSION: Dan is older than Fern.

    A. The conclusion is proved by Statements 1-4;
    B. The conclusion is disproved by Statements 1-4;
    C. The facts are not sufficient to prove or disprove the conclusion.

19.____

20. FACTUAL STATEMENTS:
    1) Each of Fred's three sofa cushions lies on top of four lost coins.
    2) The cushion on the right covers two pennies and two dimes.
    3) The middle cushion covers two dimes and two quarters.
    4) The cushion on the left covers two nickels and two quarters.

    CONCLUSION: To be guaranteed of retrieving at least one coin of each denomination, and without looking at any of the coins, Frank must take three coins each from under the cushions on the right and the left.

    A. The conclusion is proved by Statements 1-4;
    B. The conclusion is disproved by Statements 1-4;
    C. The facts are not sufficient to prove or disprove the conclusion.

20.____

21. FACTUAL STATEMENTS:
    1) The door to the hammer mill chamber is locked if light 6 is red.
    2) The door to the hammer mill chamber is locked only when the mill is operating.
    3) If the mill is not operating, light 6 is blue.
    4) The door to the hammer mill chamber is locked.

    CONCLUSION: The mill is in operation.

    A. The conclusion is proved by Statements 1-4;
    B. The conclusion is disproved by Statements 1-4;
    C. The facts are not sufficient to prove or disprove the conclusion.

21.____

22. FACTUAL STATEMENTS:
    1) In a five-story office building, where each story is occupied by a single professional, Dr. Kane's office is above Dr. Assad's.
    2) Dr. Johnson's office is between Dr. Kane's and Dr. Conlon's.
    3) Dr. Steen's office is between Dr. Conlon's and Dr. Assad's.
    4) Dr. Johnson is on the fourth story.

    CONCLUSION: Dr. Steen occupies the second story.

22.____

8 (#1)

   A. The conclusion is proved by Statements 1-4;
   B. The conclusion is disproved by Statements 1-4;
   C. The facts are not sufficient to prove or disprove the conclusion.

23. FACTUAL STATEMENTS: 23.____
    1) On Saturday, farmers Hank, Earl, Roy, and Cletus plowed a total of 520 acres.
    2) Hank plowed twice as many acres as Roy.
    3) Roy plowed half as much as the farmer who plowed the most.
    4) Cletus plowed 160 acres.

    CONCLUSION: Hank plowed 200 acres.
       A. The conclusion is proved by Statements 1-4;
       B. The conclusion is disproved by Statements 1-4;
       C. The facts are not sufficient to prove or disprove the conclusion.

24. FACTUAL STATEMENTS: 24.____
    1) Four travelers – Tina, Jodie, Alex, and Oscar – each traveled to a different island – Aruba, Jamaica, Nevis, and Barbados – but not necessarily respectively.
    2) Tina did not travel as far to Jamaica as Jodie traveled to her island.
    3) Oscar traveled twice as far as Alex, who traveled the same distance as the traveler who went to Aruba.
    4) Oscar went to Barbados.

    CONCLUSION: Oscar traveled the farthest.

       A. The conclusion is proved by Statements 1-4;
       B. The conclusion is disproved by Statements 1-4;
       C. The facts are not sufficient to prove or disprove the conclusion.

25. FACTUAL STATEMENT: 25.____
    1) In the natural history museum, every Native American display that contains pottery also contains beadwork.
    2) Some of the displays containing lodge replicas also contain beadwork.
    3) The display on the Choctaw, a Native American tribe, contains pottery.
    4) The display on the Modoc, a Native American tribe, contains only two of these items.

    CONCLUSION: If the Modoc display contains pottery, it does not contain lodge replicas.

       A. The conclusion is proved by Statements 1-4;
       B. The conclusion is disproved by Statements 1-4;
       C. The facts are not sufficient to prove or disprove the conclusion.

9 (#1)

KEY (CORRECT ANSWERS)

1.	A		11.	B
2.	B		12.	C
3.	A		13.	B
4.	A		14.	D
5.	C		15.	E
6.	B		16.	E
7.	B		17.	A
8.	B		18.	B
9.	A		19.	C
10.	B		20.	A

21. A
22. A
23. C
24. A
25. A

TEST 2

DIRECTIONS: Each question or incomplete statement is followed by several suggested answers or completions. Select the one that BEST answers the question or completes the statement. *PRINT THE LETTER OF THE CORRECT ANSWER IN THE SPACE AT THE RIGHT.*

Questions 1-9.

DIRECTIONS: In Questions 1 through 9, you will read a set of facts and a conclusion drawn from them. The conclusion may be valid or invalid, based on the facts. It is your task to determine the validity of the conclusion.
For each question, select the letter before the statement that BEST expresses the relationship between the given facts and the conclusion that has been drawn from them. Your choices are:
   A. The facts prove the conclusion.
   B. The facts disprove the conclusion; or
   C. The facts neither prove nor disprove the conclusion.

1. FACTS: If the maximum allowable income for Medicaid recipients is increased, the number of Medicaid recipients will increase. If the number of Medicaid recipients increases, more funds must be allocated to the Medicaid program, which will require a tax increase. Taxes cannot be approved without the approval of the legislature. The legislature probably will not approve a tax increase.

   CONCLUSION: The maximum allowable income for Medicaid recipients will increase.

   A. The facts prove the conclusion.
   B. The facts disprove the conclusion; or
   C. The facts neither prove nor disprove the conclusion.

1.____

2. FACTS: All the dentists on the baseball team are short. Everyone in the dugout is a dentist, but not everyone in the dugout is short. The baseball team is not made up of people of any particular profession.

   CONCLUSION: Some people who are not dentists are in the dugout.

   A. The facts prove the conclusion.
   B. The facts disprove the conclusion; or
   C. The facts neither prove nor disprove the conclusion.

2.____

3. FACTS: A taxi company's fleet is divided into two fleets. Fleet One contains cabs A, B, C, and D. Fleet Two contains E, F, G, and H. Each cab is either yellow or green. Five of the cabs are yellow. Cabs A and E are not both yellow. Either Cab C or F, or both, are not yellow. Cabs B and H are either both yellow or both green.

   CONCLUSION: Cab H is green.

3.____

144

2 (#2)

   A. The facts prove the conclusion.
   B. The facts disprove the conclusion; or
   C. The facts neither prove nor disprove the conclusion.

4. FACTS: Most people in the skydiving club are not afraid of heights. Everyone in the skydiving club makes three parachute jumps a month.

   CONCLUSION: At least one person who is afraid of heights makes three parachute jumps a month.

   A. The facts prove the conclusion.
   B. The facts disprove the conclusion; or
   C. The facts neither prove nor disprove the conclusion.

4.____

5. FACTS: If the Board approves the new rule, the agency will move to a new location immediately. If the agency moves, five new supervisors will be immediately appointed. The Board has approved the new proposal.

   CONCLUSION: No new supervisors were appointed.

   A. The facts prove the conclusion.
   B. The facts disprove the conclusion; or
   C. The facts neither prove nor disprove the conclusion.

5.____

6. FACTS: All the workers at the supermarket chew gum when they sack groceries. Sometimes Lance, a supermarket worker, doesn't chew gum at all when he works. Another supermarket worker, Jenny, chews gum the whole time she is at work.

   CONCLUSION: Jenny always sacks groceries when she is at work.

6.____

7. FACTS: Lake Lottawatta is bigger than Lake Tacomi. Lake Tacomi and Lake Ottawa are exactly the same size. All lakes in Montana are bigger than Lake Ottawa.

   CONCLUSION: Lake Lottawatta is in Montana.

   A. The facts prove the conclusion.
   B. The facts disprove the conclusion; or
   C. The facts neither prove nor disprove the conclusion.

7.____

8. FACTS: Two men, Cox and Taylor, are playing poker at a table. Taylor has a pair of aces in his hand. One man is smoking a cigar. One of them has no pairs in his hand and is wearing an eye patch. The man wearing the eye patch is smoking a cigar. One man is bald.

   CONCLUSION: Cox is smoking a cigar.

8.____

A. The facts prove the conclusion.
B. The facts disprove the conclusion; or
C. The facts neither prove nor disprove the conclusion.

9. FACTS: All Kwakiutls are Wakashan Indians. All Wakashan Indians originated on Vancouver Island. The Nootka also originated on Vancouver Island.

   CONCLUSION: Kwakiutls originated on Vancouver Island.

   A. The facts prove the conclusion.
   B. The facts disprove the conclusion; or
   C. The facts neither prove nor disprove the conclusion.

9.____

Questions 10-17.

DIRECTIONS: Questions 10 through 17 are based on the following reading passage. It is not your knowledge of the particular topic that is being tested, but your ability to reason based on what you have read. The passage is likely to detail several proposed courses of action and factors affecting these proposals. The reading passage is followed by a conclusion or outcome based on the facts in the passage, or a description of a decision taken regarding the situation. The conclusion is followed by a number of statements that have a possible connection to the conclusion. For each statement, you are to determine whether:
A. The statement proves the conclusion.
B. The statement supports the conclusion but does not prove it.
C. The statement disproves the conclusion.
D. The statement weakens the conclusion but does not disprove it.
E. The statement has no relevance to the conclusion.

Remember that the conclusion after the passage is to be accepted as the outcome of what actually happened, and that you are being asked to evaluate the impact each statement would have had on the conclusion.

PASSAGE

The World Wide Web portal and search engine, HipBot, is considering becoming a subscription-only service, locking out nonsubscribers from the content on its web site. HipBot currently relies solely on advertising revenues.

HipBot's content director says that by taking in an annual fee from each customer, the company can both increase profits and provide premium content that no other portal can match.

The marketing director disagrees, saying that there is no guarantee that anyone who now visits the web site for free will agree to pay for the privilege of visiting it again. Most will probably simply use the other major portals. Also, HipBot's advertising clients will not be happy when they learn that the site will be viewed by a more limited number of people.

4 (#2)

CONCLUSION: In January of 2016, the CEO of HipBot decides to keep the portal open to all web users, with some limited "premium content" available to subscribers who don't mind paying a little extra to access it. The company will aim to maintain, or perhaps increase, its advertising revenue.

10. In an independent marketing survey, 62% of respondents said they "strongly agree" with the following statement: "I almost never pay attention to advertisements that appear on the World Wide Web."
    A. The statement proves the conclusion.
    B. The statement supports the conclusion but does not prove it.
    C. The statement disproves the conclusion.
    D. The statement weakens the conclusion but does not disprove it.
    E. The statement has no relevance to the conclusion.

    10.____

11. When it learns about the subscription-only debate going on at HipBot, Wernham Hogg Entertainment, one of HipBot's most reliable clients, says it will withdraw its ads and place them on a free web portal if HipBot decides to limit its content to subscribers. Wernham Hogg pays HipBot about $6 million annually – about 12% of HipBot's gross revenues – to run its ads online.
    A. The statement proves the conclusion.
    B. The statement supports the conclusion but does not prove it.
    C. The statement disproves the conclusion.
    D. The statement weakens the conclusion but does not disprove it.
    E. The statement has no relevance to the conclusion.

    11.____

12. At the end of the second quarter of FY 2016, after continued stagnant profits, the CEO of HipBot assembles a blue ribbon commission to gather and analyze data on the costs, benefits, and feasibility of adding a limited amount of "premium" content to the HipBot portal.
    A. The statement proves the conclusion.
    B. The statement supports the conclusion but does not prove it.
    C. The statement disproves the conclusion.
    D. The statement weakens the conclusion but does not disprove it.
    E. The statement has no relevance to the conclusion.

    12.____

13. In the following fiscal year, Wernham Hogg Entertainment, satisfied with the "hit counts" on HipBot's free web site, spends another $1 million on advertisements that will appear on web pages that are available to HipBot's "premium subscribers.
    A. The statement proves the conclusion.
    B. The statement supports the conclusion but does not prove it.
    C. The statement disproves the conclusion.
    D. The statement weakens the conclusion but does not disprove it.
    E. The statement has no relevance to the conclusion.

    13.____

14. HipBot's information technology director reports that the engineers in his department have come up with a feature that will search not only individual web pages, but tie into other web-based search engines, as well, and then comb through all these results to find those most relevant to the user's search.

    14.____

A. The statement proves the conclusion.
B. The statement supports the conclusion but does not prove it.
C. The statement disproves the conclusion.
D. The statement weakens the conclusion but does not disprove it.
E. The statement has no relevance to the conclusion.

15. In an independent marketing survey, 79% of respondents said they "strongly agree" with the following statement: "Many web sites are so dominated by advertisements these days that it is increasingly frustrating to find the content I want to read or see."
    A. The statement proves the conclusion.
    B. The statement supports the conclusion but does not prove it.
    C. The statement disproves the conclusion.
    D. The statement weakens the conclusion but does not disprove it.
    E. The statement has no relevance to the conclusion.

15.____

16. After three years of studies at the federal level, the Department of Commerce releases a report suggesting that, in general, the only private "subscriber-only" web sites that do well financially are those with a very specialized user population.
    A. The statement proves the conclusion.
    B. The statement supports the conclusion but does not prove it.
    C. The statement disproves the conclusion.
    D. The statement weakens the conclusion but does not disprove it.
    E. The statement has no relevance to the conclusion.

16.____

17. HipBot's own marketing research indicates that the introduction of premium content has the potential to attract new users to the HipBot portal.
    A. The statement proves the conclusion.
    B. The statement supports the conclusion but does not prove it.
    C. The statement disproves the conclusion.
    D. The statement weakens the conclusion but does not disprove it.
    E. The statement has no relevance to the conclusion.

17.____

Questions 18-25.

DIRECTIONS: Questions 18 through 25 each provide four factual statements and a conclusion based on these statements. After reading the entire question, you will decide whether:
A. The conclusion is proved by Statements 1-4;
B. The conclusion is disproved by Statements 1-4;
C. The facts are not sufficient to prove or disprove the conclusion.

6 (#2)

18. FACTUAL STATEMENTS:
   1) If the alarm goes off, Sam will wake up.
   2) If Tandy wakes up before 4:00, Linda will leave the bedroom and sleep on the couch.
   3) If Linda leaves the bedroom, she'll check the alarm to make sure it is working.
   4) The alarm goes off.

   CONCLUSION: Tandy woke up before 4:00.

   A. The conclusion is proved by Statements 1-4;
   B. The conclusion is disproved by Statements 1-4;
   C. The facts are not sufficient to prove or disprove the conclusion.

18.____

19. FACTUAL STATEMENTS:
   1) Four brothers are named Earl, John, Gary, and Pete.
   2) Earl and Pete are unmarried.
   3) John is shorter than the youngest of the four.
   4) The oldest brother is married, and is also the tallest.

   CONCLUSION: Pete is the youngest brother.

   A. The conclusion is proved by Statements 1-4;
   B. The conclusion is disproved by Statements 1-4;
   C. The facts are not sufficient to prove or disprove the conclusion.

19.____

20. FACTUAL STATEMENTS:
   1) Automobile engines are cooled either by air or by liquid.
   2) If the engine is small and simple enough, air from a belt-driven fan will cool it sufficiently.
   3) Most newer automobile engines are too complicated to be air-cooled.
   4) Air-cooled engines are cheaper and easier to build then liquid-cooled engines.

   CONCLUSION: Most newer automobile engines use liquid coolant.

   A. The conclusion is proved by Statements 1-4;
   B. The conclusion is disproved by Statements 1-4;
   C. The facts are not sufficient to prove or disprove the conclusion.

20.____

21. FACTUAL STATEMENTS:
   1) Erica will only file a lawsuit if she is injured while parasailing.
   2) If Rick orders Trip to run a rope test, Trip will check the rigging.
   3) If the rigging does not malfunction, Erica will not be injured.
   4) Rick orders Trip to run a rope test.

21.____

7 (#2)

CONCLUSION: Erica does not file a lawsuit.

- A. The conclusion is proved by Statements 1-4;
- B. The conclusion is disproved by Statements 1-4;
- C. The facts are not sufficient to prove or disprove the conclusion.

22. FACTUAL STATEMENTS:
    1) On Maple Street, which is four blocks long, Bill's shop is two blocks east of Ken's shop.
    2) Ken's shop is one block west of the only shop on Maple Street with an awning.
    3) Erma's shop is one block west of the easternmost block.
    4) Bill's shop is on the easternmost block.

    CONCLUSION: Bill's shop has an awning.

    - A. The conclusion is proved by Statements 1-4;
    - B. The conclusion is disproved by Statements 1-4;
    - C. The facts are not sufficient to prove or disprove the conclusion.

23. FACTUAL STATEMENTS:
    1) Gear X rotates in a clockwise direction if Switch C is in the OFF position.
    2) Gear X will rotate in a counter-clockwise direction if Switch C is ON.
    3) If Gear X is rotating in a clockwise direction, then Gear Y will not be rotating at all.
    4) Gear Y is rotating.

    CONCLUSION: Gear X is rotating in a counter-clockwise direction.

    - A. The conclusion is proved by Statements 1-4;
    - B. The conclusion is disproved by Statements 1-4;
    - C. The facts are not sufficient to prove or disprove the conclusion.

24. FACTUAL STATEMENTS:
    1) The Republic of Garbanzo's currency system has four basic denominations: the pastor, the noble, the donner, and the rojo.
    2) A pastor is worth 2 nobles.
    3) 2 donners can be exchanged for a rojo.
    4) 3 pastors are equal in value to 2 donners.

    CONCLUSION: The rojo is most valuable.

    - A. The conclusion is proved by Statements 1-4;
    - B. The conclusion is disproved by Statements 1-4;
    - C. The facts are not sufficient to prove or disprove the conclusion.

8 (#2)

25. FACTUAL STATEMENTS:
   1) At Prickett's Nursery, the only citrus trees left are either Meyer lemons or Valencia oranges, and every citrus tree left is either a dwarf or a semidwarf.
   2) Half of the semidwarf trees are Meyer lemons.
   3) There are more semidwarf trees left than dwarf trees.
   4) A quarter of the dwarf trees are Valencia oranges.

   CONCLUSION: There are more Valencia oranges left at Prickett's Nursery than Meyer lemons.

   A. The conclusion is proved by Statements 1-4;
   B. The conclusion is disproved by Statements 1-4;
   C. The facts are not sufficient to prove or disprove the conclusion.

   25.____

KEY (CORRECT ANSWERS)

1. C
2. B
3. B
4. A
5. B

6. C
7. C
8. A
9. A
10. E

11. B
12. C
13. A
14. E
15. D

16. B
17. B
18. C
19. C
20. A

21. C
22. B
23. C
24. A
25. B

PREPARING WRITTEN MATERIAL

PARAGRAPH REARRANGEMENT
COMMENTARY

The sentences that follow are in scrambled order. You are to rearrange them in proper order and indicate the letter choice containing the correct answer at the space at the right.

Each group of sentences in this section is actually a paragraph presented in scrambled order. Each sentence in the group has a place in that paragraph; no sentence is to be left out. You are to read each group of sentences and decide upon the best order in which to put the sentences so as to form a well-organized paragraph.

The questions in this section measure the ability to solve a problem when all the facts relevant to its solution are not given.

More specifically, certain positions of responsibility and authority require the employee to discover connection between events sometimes, apparently, unrelated. In order to do this, the employee will find it necessary to correctly infer that unspecified events have probably occurred or are likely to occur. This ability becomes especially important when action must be taken on incomplete information.

Accordingly, these questions require competitors to choose among several suggested alternatives, each of which presents a different sequential arrangement of the events. Competitors must choose the MOST logical of the suggested sequences.

In order to do so, they may be required to draw on general knowledge to infer missing concepts or events that are essential to sequencing the given events. Competitors should be careful to infer only what is essential to the sequence. The plausibility of the wrong alternatives will always require the inclusion of unlikely events or of additional chains of events which are NOT essential to sequencing the given events.

It's very important to remember that you are looking for the best of the four possible choices, and that the best choice of all may not even be one of the answers you're given to choose from.

There is no one right way to solve these problems. Many people have found it helpful to first write out the order of the sentences, as they would have arranged them, on their scrap paper before looking at the possible answers. If their optimum answer is there, this can save them some time. If it isn't, this method can still give insight into solving the problem. Others find it most helpful to just go through each of the possible choices, contrasting each as they go along. You should use whatever method feels comfortable and works for you.

While most of these types of questions are not that difficult, we've added a higher percentage of the difficult type, just to give you more practice. Usually there are only one or two questions on this section that contain such subtle distinctions that you're unable to answer confidently. And you then may find yourself stuck deciding between two possible choices, neither of which you're sure about.

EXAMINATION SECTION
TEST 1

DIRECTIONS: The sentences that follow are in scrambled order. You are to rearrange them in proper order and indicate the letter choice containing the correct answer. *PRINT THE LETTER OF THE CORRECT ANSWER IN THE SPACE AT THE RIGHT.*

1. Below are four statements labeled W, X, Y and Z.
   W. He was a strict and fanatic drillmaster.
   X. The word is always used in a derogatory sense and generally shows resentment and anger on the part of the user.
   Y. It is from the name of this Frenchman that we derive our English word, martinet.
   Z. Jean Martinet was the Inspector-General of Infantry during the reign of King Louis XIV.
   The PROPER order in which these sentences should be placed in a paragraph is:
   A. X, Z, W, Y   B. X, Z, Y, W   C. Z, W, Y, X   D. Z, Y, W, X

   1.____

2. In the following paragraph, the sentences, which are numbered, have been jumbled.
   I. Since then it has undergone changes.
   II. It was incorporated in 1955 under the laws of the State of New York.
   III. Its primary purposes, a cleaner city, has, however, remained the same.
   IV. The Citizens Committee works in cooperation with the Mayor's Inter-departmental Committee for a Clean City.
   The order in which these sentences should be arranged to form a well-organized paragraph is:
   A. II, IV, I, III   B. III, IV, I, II   C. IV, II, I, III   D. IV, III, II, I

   2.____

   3.____

Questions 3-5.

DIRECTIONS: The sentences listed below are part of a meaningful paragraph but they are not given in their proper order. You are to decide what would be the BEST order in which to put the sentences so as to form a well-organized paragraph. Each sentence has a place in the paragraph; there are no extra sentences. You are then to answer Questions 3 through 5 inclusive on the basis of your rearrangements of these scrambled sentences into a properly organized paragraph.

In 1887 some insurance companies organized an Inspection Department to advise their clients on all phases of fire prevention and protection. Probably this has been due to the smaller annual fire losses in Great Britain than in the United States. It tests various fire prevention devices and appliances and determines manufacturing hazards and their safeguards. Fire research began earlier in the United States and is more advanced than in Great Britain. Later they established a laboratory specializing in electrical, mechanical, hydraulic, and chemical fields.

155

2 (#1)

3. When the five sentences are arranged in proper order, the paragraph starts with the sentence which begins 3._____
   A. "In 1887…" B. "Probably this…" C. "It tests…"
   D. "Fire research…" E. "Later they…"

4. In the last sentence listed above, "they" refers to 4._____
   A. the insurance companies B. the United States and Great Britain
   C. the Inspection Department D. clients
   E. technicians

5. When the above paragraph is properly arranged, it ends with the words 5._____
   A. "…and protection." B. "…the United States."
   C. "…their safeguards." D. "…in Great Britain."
   E. "…chemical fields."

KEY (CORRECT ANSWERS)

1. C
2. C
3. D
4. A
5. C

TEST 2

DIRECTIONS: In each of the questions numbered I through V, several sentences are given. For each question, choose as your answer the group of number that represents the MOST logical order of these sentences if they were arranged in paragraph form. *PRINT THE LETTER OF THE CORRECT ANSWER IN THE SPACE AT THE RIGHT.*

1.
   I. It is established when one shows that the landlord has prevented the tenant's enjoyment of his interest in the property leased.
   II. Constructive eviction is the result of a breach of the covenant of quiet enjoyment implied in all leases.
   III. In some parts of the United States, it is not complete until the tenant vacates within a reasonable time.
   IV. Generally, the acts must be of such serious and permanent character as to deny the tenant the enjoyment of his possessing rights.
   V. In this event, upon abandonment of the premises, the tenant's liability for that ceases.
   The CORRECT answer is:
   A. II, I, IV, III, V
   B. V, II, III, I, IV
   C. IV, III, I, II, V
   D. I, III, V, IV, II

   1.____

2.
   I. The powerlessness before private and public authorities that is the typical experience of the slum tenant is reminiscent of the situation of blue-collar workers all through the nineteenth century.
   II. Similarly, in recent years, this chapter of history has been reopened by anti-poverty groups which have attempted to organize slum tenants to enable them to bargain collectively with their landlords about the conditions of their tenancies.
   III. It is familiar history that many of the worker remedied their condition by joining together and presenting their demands collectively.
   IV. Like the workers, tenants are forced by the conditions of modern life into substantial dependence on these who possess great political aid and economic power.
   V. What's more, the very fact of dependence coupled with an absence of education and self-confidence makes them hesitant and unable to stand up for what they need from those in power.
   The CORRECT answer is:
   A. V, IV, I, II, III
   B. II, III, I, V, IV
   C. III, I, V, IV, II
   D. I, IV, V, III, II

   2.____

3.
   I. A railroad, for example, when not acting as a common carrier may contract away responsibility for its own negligence.
   II. As to a landlord, however, no decision has been found relating to the legal effect of a clause shifting the statutory duty of repair to the tenant.
   III. The courts have not passed on the validity of clauses relieving the landlord of this duty and liability.
   IV. They have, however, upheld the validity of exculpatory clauses in other types of contracts.

   3.____

157

V. Housing regulations impose a duty upon the landlord to maintain leased premises in safe condition.
VI. As another example, a bailee may limit his liability except for gross negligence, willful acts, or fraud.

The CORRECT answer is:
A. II, I, VI, IV, III, V
B. I, III, IV, V, VI, II
C. III, V, I, IV, II, VI
D. V, III, IV, I, VI, II

4. I. Since there are only samples in the building, retail or consumer sales are generally eschewed by mart occupants, and in some instances, rigid controls are maintained to limit entrance to the mart only to those persons engaged in retailing.
    II. Since World War I, in many larger cities, there has developed a new type of property, called the mart building.
    III. It can, therefore, be used by wholesalers and jobbers for the display of sample merchandise.
    IV. This type of building is most frequently a multi-storied, finished interior property which is a cross between a retail arcade and a loft building.
    V. This limitation enables the mart occupants to ship the orders from another location after the retailer or dealer makes his selection from the samples.

    The CORRECT answer is:
    A. II, IV, III, I, V
    B. IV, III, V, I, II
    C. I, III, II, IV, V
    D. I, IV, II, III, V

5. I. In general, staff-line friction reduces the distinctive contribution of staff personnel.
    II. The conflicts, however, introduce an uncontrolled element into the managerial system.
    III. On the other hand, the natural resistance of the line to staff innovations probably usefully restrains over-eager efforts to apply untested procedures on a large scale.
    IV. Under such conditions, it is difficult to know when valuable ideas are being sacrificed.
    V. The relatively weak position of staff, requiring accommodation to the line, tends to restrict their ability to engage in free, experimental innovation.

    The CORRECT answer is:
    A. IV, II, III, I, V
    B. I, V, III, II, IV
    C. V, III, I, II, IV
    D. II, I, IV, V, III

KEY (CORRECT ANSWERS)

1. A
2. D
3. D
4. A
5. B

TEST 3

DIRECTIONS: Questions 1 through 4 consist of six sentences which can be arranged in a logical sequence. For each question, select the choice which places the numbered sentences in the MOST logical sequent. *PRINT THE LETTER OF THE CORRECT ANSWER IN THE SPACE AT THE RIGHT.*

1.
   I. The burden of proof as to each issue is determined before trial and remains upon the same party throughout the trial.
   II. The jury is at liberty to believe one witness' testimony as against a number of contradictory witnesses.
   III. In a civil case, the party bearing the burden of proof is required to prove his contention by a fair preponderance of the evidence.
   IV. However, it must be noted that a fair preponderance of evidence does not necessarily mean a greater number of witnesses.
   V. The burden of proof is the burden which rests upon one of the parties to an action to persuade the trier of the facts, generally the jury, that a proposition he asserts is true.
   VI. If the evidence is equally balanced, or if it leaves the jury in such doubt as to be unable to decide the controversy either way, judgment must be given against the party upon whom the burden of proof rests.
   The CORRECT answer is:
   A. III, II, V, IV, I, VI
   B. I, II, VI, V, III, IV
   C. III, IV, V, I, II, VI
   D. V, I, III, VI, IV, II

1.____

2.
   I. If a parent is without assets and is unemployed, he cannot be convicted of the crime of non-support of a child.
   II. The term "sufficient ability" has been held to mean sufficient financial ability.
   III. It does not matter if his unemployment is by choice or unavoidable circumstances.
   IV. If he fails to take any steps at all, he may be liable to prosecution for endangering the welfare of a child.
   V. Under the penal law, a parent is responsible for the support of his minor child only if the parent is "of sufficient ability."
   VI. An indigent parent may meet his obligation by borrowing money or by seeking aid under the provisions of the Social Welfare Law.
   The CORRECT answer is:
   A. VI, I, V, III, II, IV
   B. I, III, V, II, IV, VI
   C. V, II, I, III, VI, IV
   D. I, VI, IV, V, II, III

2.____

3.
   I. Consider, for example, the case of a rabble rouser who urges a group of twenty people to go out and break the windows of a nearby factory.
   II. Therefore, the law fills the indicated gap with the crime of inciting to riot.
   III. A person is considered guilty of inciting to riot when he urges ten or more persons to engage in tumultuous and violent conduct of a kind likely to create public alarm.
   IV. However, if he has not obtained the cooperation of at least four people, he cannot be charged with unlawful assembly.

3.____

2 (#3)

V. The charge of inciting to riot was added to the law to cover types of conduct which cannot be classified as either the crime of "riot" or the crime of "unlawful assembly."
VI. If he acquires the acquiescence of at least four of them, he is guilty of unlawful assembly even if the project does not materialize.

The CORRECT answer is:
A. III, V, I, VI, IV, II
B. V, I, IV, VI, II, III
C. III, IV, I, V, II, VI
D. V, I, IV, VI, III, II

4. I. If, however, the rebuttal evidence presents an issue of credibility, it is for the jury to determine whether the presumption has, in fact, been destroyed.
II. Once sufficient evidence to the contrary is introduced, the presumption disappears from the trial.
III. The effect of a presumption is to place the burden upon the adversary to come forward with evidence to rebut the presumption.
IV. When a presumption is overcome and ceases to exist in the case, the fact or facts which gave rise to the presumption still remain.
V. Whether a presumption has been overcome is ordinarily a question for the court.
VI. Such information may furnish a basis for a logical inference.

The CORRECT answer is:
A. IV, VI, II, V, I, III
B. III, II, V, I, IV, VI
C. V, III, VI, IV, II, I
D. V, IV, I, II, VI, III

4.____

KEY (CORRECT ANSWERS)

1. D
2. C
3. A
4. B

PREPARING WRITTEN MATERIAL
EXAMINATION SECTION
TEST 1

Questions 1-15.

DIRECTIONS: For each of Questions 1 through 15, select from the options given below the MOST applicable choice, and mark your answer accordingly.
    A. The sentence is correct.
    B. The sentence contains a spelling error only.
    C. The sentence contains an English grammar error only.
    D. The sentence contains both a spelling error and an English grammar error.

1. He is a very dependable person whom we expect will be an asset to this division. 1.____

2. An investigator often finds it necessary to be very diplomatic when conducting an interview. 2.____

3. Accurate detail is especially important if court action results from an investigation. 3.____

4. The report was signed by him and I since we conducted the investigation jointly. 4.____

5. Upon receipt of the complaint, an inquiry was begun. 5.____

6. An employee has to organize his time so that he can handle his workload efficiantly. 6.____

7. It was not apparent that anyone was living at the address given by the client. 7.____

8. According to regulations, there is to be at least three attempts made to locate the client. 8.____

9. Neither the inmate nor the correction officer was willing to sign a formal statement. 9.____

10. It is our opinion that one of the persons interviewed were lying. 10.____

11. We interviewed both clients and departmental personel in the course of this investigation. 11.____

12. It is concievable that further research might produce additional evidence. 12.____

13. There are too many occurences of this nature to ignore. 13.____

161

2 (#1)

14. We cannot accede to the candidate's request.   14._____

15. The submission of overdue reports is the reason that there was a delay in   15._____
    completion of this investigation.

Questions 16-25.

DIRECTIONS: Each of Questions 16 through 25 may be classified under one of the following
            four categories:
                A. Faulty because of incorrect grammar or sentence structure.
                B. Faulty because of incorrect punctuation.
                C. Faulty because of incorrect spelling.
                D. Correct

            Examine each sentence carefully to determine under which of the above four
            options it is best classified. Then, in the space at the right, write the letter
            preceding the option which is the BEST of the four suggested above. Each
            incorrect sentence contains but one type of error. Consider a sentence to be
            correct if it contains none of the types of errors mentioned, even though there
            may be other correct ways of expressing the same thought.

16. Although the department's supply of scratch pads and stationary have   16._____
    diminished considerably, the allotment for our division has not been reduced.

17. You have not told us whom you wish to designate as your secretary.   17._____

18. Upon reading the minutes of the last meeting, the new proposal was taken   18._____
    up for consideration.

19. Before beginning the discussion, we locked the door as a precautionery   19._____
    measure.

20. The supervisor remarked, "Only those clerks, who perform routine work,   20._____
    are permitted to take a rest period."

21. Not only will this duplicating machine make accurate copies, but it will also   21._____
    produce a quantity of work equal to fifteen transcribing typists.

22. "Mr. Jones," said the supervisor, "we regret our inability to grant you an   22._____
    extention of your leave of absence.

23. Although the employees find the work monotonous and fatigueing, they   23._____
    rarely complain.

24. We completed the tabulation of the receipts on time despite the fact that   24._____
    Miss Smith our fastest operator was absent for over a week.

25. The reaction of the employees who attended the meeting, as well as the reaction of those who did not attend, indicates clearly that the schedule is satisfactory to everyone concerned.

25._____

KEY (CORRECT ANSWERS)

1.	D		11.	B
2.	A		12.	B
3.	A		13.	B
4.	C		14.	A
5.	A		15.	C
6.	B		16.	A
7.	B		17.	D
8.	C		18.	A
9.	A		19.	C
10.	C		20.	B

21. A
22. C
23. C
24. B
25. D

TEST 2

Questions 1-15.

DIRECTIONS: Questions 1 through 15 consist of two sentences. Some are correct according to ordinary formal English usage. Others are incorrect because they contain errors in English usage, spelling, or punctuation. Consider a sentence correct if it contains no errors in English usage, spelling, or punctuation, even if there may be other ways of writing the sentence correctly. Mark your answer:
- A. If only sentence I is correct.
- B. If only sentence II is correct.
- C. If sentences 1 and II are correct.
- D. If neither sentence I nor II is correct.

1. I. The influence of recruitment efficiency upon administrative standards is readily apparant.
   II. Rapid and accurate thinking are an essential quality of the police officer.

2. I. The administrator of a police department is constantly confronted by the demands of subordinates for increased personnel in their respective units.
   II. Since a chief executive must work within well-defined fiscal limits, he must weigh the relative importance of various requests.

3. I. The two men whom the police arrested for a parking violation were wanted for robbery in three states.
   II. Strong executive control from the top to the bottom of the enterprise is one of the basic principals of police administration.

4. I. When he gave testimony unfavorable to the defendant loyalty seemed to mean very little.
   II. Having run off the road while passing a car, the patrolman gave the driver a traffic ticket.

5. I. The judge ruled that the defendant's conversation with his doctor was a privileged communication.
   II. The importance of our training program is widely recognized; however, fiscal difficulties limit the program's effectiveness.

6. I. Despite an increase in patrol coverage, there were less arrests for crimes against property this year.
   II. The investigators could hardly have expected greater cooperation from the public.

7. I. Neither the patrolman nor the witness could identify the defendant as the driver of the car.
   II. Each of the officers in the class received their certificates at the completion of the course.

8. I. The new commander made it clear that those kind of procedures would no longer be permitted.
   II. Giving some weight to performance records is more advisable than making promotions solely on the basis of test scores.

8._____

9. I. A deputy sheriff must ascertain whether the debtor, has any property.
   II. A good deputy sheriff does not cause histerical excitement when he executes a process.

9._____

10. I. Having learned that he has been assigned a judgment debtor, the deputy sheriff should call upon him.
    II. The deputy sheriff may seize and remove property without requiring a bond.

10._____

11. I. If legal procedures are not observed, the resulting contract is not enforseable.
    II. If the directions from the creditor's attorney are not in writing, the deputy sheriff should request a letter of instructions from the attorney.

11._____

12. I. The deputy sheriff may confer with the defendant and enter this defendants' place of business.
    II. A deputy sheriff must ascertain from the creditor's attorney whether the debtor has any property against which he may proceede.

12._____

13. I. The sheriff has a right to do whatever is necessary for the purpose of executing the order of the court.
    II. The written order of the court gives the sheriff general authority and he is governed in his acts by a very simple principal.

13._____

14. I. Either the patrolman or his sergeant are always ready to help the public.
    II. The sergeant asked the patrolman when he would finish the report.

14._____

15. I. The injured man could not hardly talk.
    II. Every officer had ought to had in their reports on time.

15._____

Questions 16-26.

DIRECTIONS: For each of the sentences given below, numbered 16 through 25, select from the following choices the MOST correct choice and print your choice in the space at the right. Select as your answer:
A. If the statement contains an unnecessary word or expression
B. If the statement contains a slang term or expression ordinarily not acceptable in government report writing.
C. If the statement contains an old-fashioned word or expression, where a concrete, plain term would be more useful.
D. If the statement contains no major faults.

16. Every one of us should try harder.

16._____

17. Yours of the first instant has been received.

17._____

3 (#2)

18. We will have to do a real snow job on him.   18._____
19. I shall contact him next Thursday.   19._____
20. None of us were invited to the meeting with the community.   20._____
21. We got this here job to do.   21._____
22. She could not help but see the mistake in the checkbook.   22._____
23. Don't bug the Director about the report.   23._____
24. I beg to inform you that your letter has been received.   24._____
25. This project is all screwed up.   25._____

KEY (CORRECT ANSWERS)

1.	D		11.	B
2.	C		12.	D
3.	A		13.	A
4.	D		14.	D
5.	B		15.	D
6.	B		16.	D
7.	A		17.	C
8.	D		18.	B
9.	D		19.	D
10.	C		20.	D

21. B
22. D
23. B
24. C
25. B

TEST 3

DIRECTIONS: Questions 1 through 25 are sentences taken from reports. Some are correct according to ordinary English usage. Others are incorrect because they contain errors in English usage, spelling, or punctuation. Consider a sentence correct if it contains no errors in English usage, spelling, or punctuation, even if there may be other ways of writing the sentence correctly. Mark your answer:
- A. If only sentence I is correct
- B. If only sentence II is correct
- C. If sentences I and II are correct
- D. If neither sentence I nor II is correct

1.
   I. The Neighborhood Police Team Commander and Team Patrolmen are encouraged to give to the public the widest possible verbal and written disemination of information regarding the existence and purposes of the program.
   II. The police must be vitally interelated with every segment of the public they serve.

2.
   I. If social gambling, prostitution, and other vices are to be prohibited, the law makers should provide the manpower and method for enforcement.
   II. In addition to checking on possible crime locations such as hallways, roofs yards and other similar locations, Team Patrolmen are encouraged to make known their presence to members of the community.

3.
   I. The Neighborhood Police Team Commander is authorized to secure, the cooperation of local publications, as well as public and private agencies, to further the goals of the program.
   II. Recruitment from social minorities is essential to effective police work among minorities and meaningful relations with them.

4.
   I. The Neighborhood Police Team Commander and his men have the responsibility for providing patrol service within the sector territory on a twenty-four hour basis.
   II. While the patrolman was walking his beat at midnight he noticed that the clothing stores' door was partly open.

5.
   I. Authority is granted to the Neighborhood Police Team to device tactics for coping with the crime in the sector.
   II. Before leaving the scene of the accident, the patrolman drew a map showing the positions of the automobiles and indicated the time of the accident as 10 M. in the morning.

6.
   I. The Neighborhood Police Team Commander and his men must be kept apprised of conditions effecting their sector.
   II. Clear, continuous communication with every segment of the public served based on the realization of mutual need and founded on trust and confidence is the basis for effective law enforcement.

7. I. The irony is that the police are blamed for the laws they enforce when they are doing their duty.   7.____
   II. The Neighborhood Police Team Commander is authorized to prepare and distribute literature with pertinent information telling the public whom to contact for assistance.

8. I. The day is not far distant when major parts of the entire police compliment will need extensive college training or degrees.   8.____
   II. Although driving under the influence of alcohol is a specific charge in making arrests, drunkenness is basically a health and social problem.

9. I. If a deputy sheriff finds that property he has to attach is located on a ship, he should notify his supervisor.   9.____
   II. Any contract that tends to interfere with the administration of justice is illegal.

10. I. A mandate or official order of the court to the sheriff or other officer directs it to take into possession property of the judgment debtor.   10.____
    II. Tenancies from month-to-month, week-to-week, and sometimes year-to-year are termenable.

11. I. A civil arrest is an arrest pursuant to an order issued by a court in civil litigation.   11.____
    II. In a criminal arrest, a defendant is arrested for a crime he is alleged to have committed.

12. I. Having taken a defendant into custody, there is a complete restraint of personal liberty.   12.____
    II. Actual force is unnecessary when a deputy sheriff makes an arrest.

13. I. When a husband breaches a separation agreement by failing to supply to the wife the amount of money to be paid to her periodically under the agreement, the same legal steps may be taken to enforce his compliance as in any other breach of contract.   13.____
    II. Having obtained the writ of attachment, the plaintiff is then in the advantageous position of selling the very property that has been held for him by the sheriff while he was obtaining a judgment.

14. I. Being locked in his desk, the investigator felt sure that the records would be safe.   14.____
    II. The reason why the witness changed his statement was because he had been threatened.

15. I. The investigation had just began then an important witness disappeared.   15.____
    II. The check that had been missing was located and returned to its owner, Harry Morgan, a resident of Suffolk County, New York.

16. I. A supervisor will find that the establishment of standard procedures enables his staff to work more efficiently.
    II. An investigator hadn't ought to give any recommendations in his report if he is in doubt.

17. I. Neither the investigator nor his supervisor is ready to interview the witness.
    II. Interviewing has been and always will be an important asset in investigation.

18. I. One of the investigator's reports has been forwarded to the wrong person.
    II. The investigator stated that he was not familiar with those kind of cases.

19. I. Approaching the victim of the assault, two large bruises were noticed by me.
    II. The prisoner was arrested for assault, resisting arrest, and use of a deadly weapon.

20. I. A copy of the orders, which had been prepared by the captain, was given to each patrolman.
    II. It's always necessary to inform an arrested person of his constitutional rights before asking him any questions.

21. I. To prevent further bleeding, I applied a tourniquet to the wound.
    II. John Rano a senior officer was on duty at the time of the accident.

22. I. Limiting the term "property" to tangible property, in the criminal mischief setting, accords with prior case law holding that only tangible property came within the purview of the offense of malicious mischief.
    II. Thus, a person who intentionally destroys the property of another, but under an honest belief that he has title to such property, cannot be convicted of criminal mischief under the Revised Penal Law.

23. I. Very early in it's history, New York enacted statutes from time to time punishing, either as a felony or as a misdemeanor, malicious injuries to various kinds of property: piers, boos, dams, bridges, etc.
    II. The application of the statute is necessarily restricted to trespassory takings with larcenous intent: namely with intent permanently or virtually permanently to "appropriate" property or "deprive" the owner of its use.

24. I. Since the former Penal Law did not define the instruments of forgery in a general fashion, its crime of forgery was held to be narrower than the common law offense in this respect and to embrace only those instruments explicitly specified in the substantive provisions.
    II. After entering the barn through an open door for the purpose of stealing, it was closed by the defendants.

25. I. The use of fire or explosives to destroy tangible property is proscribed by the criminal mischief provisions of the Revised Penal Law.
    II. The defendant's taking of a taxicab for the immediate purpose of affecting his escape did not constitute grand larceny.

25._____

KEY (CORRECT ANSWERS)

1. D
2. D
3. B
4. A
5. D

6. D
7. C
8. D
9. C
10. D

11. C
12. B
13. C
14. D
15. B

16. A
17. C
18. A
19. B
20. C

21. A
22. C
23. B
24. A
25. A

TEST 4

Questions 1-4.

DIRECTIONS: Each of the two sentences in Questions 1 through 4 may be correct or may contain errors in punctuation, capitalization, or grammar. Mark your answer:
   A. If there is an error only in sentence I
   B. If there is an error only in sentence II
   C. If there is an error in both sentences I and II
   D. If both sentences are correct.

1. I. It is very annoying to have a pencil sharpener, which is not in working order.   1.____
    II. Patrolman Blake checked the door of Joe's Restaurant and found that the lock has been jammed.

2. I. When you are studying a good textbook is important.   2.____
    II. He said he would divide the money equally between you and me.

3. I. Since he went on the city council a year ago, one of his primary concerns has been safety in the streets.   3.____
    II. After waiting in the doorway for about 15 minutes, a black sedan appeared.

Questions 4-8.

DIRECTIONS: Each of the sentences in Questions 4 through 8 may be classified under one of the following four categories:
   A. Faulty because of incorrect grammar
   B. Faulty because of incorrect punctuation
   C. Faulty because of incorrect capitalization or incorrect spelling
   D. Correct

Examine each sentence carefully to determine under which of the above four options it is BEST classified. Then, in the space at the right, print the capitalized letter preceding the option which is the BEST of the four suggested above. Each faulty sentence contains but one type of error. Consider a sentence to be correct if it contains none of the types of errors mentioned, even though there may be other correct ways of expressing the same thought.

4. They told both he and I that the prisoner had escaped.   4.____

5. Any superior officer, who, disregards the just complaints of his subordinates, is remiss in the performance of his duty.   5.____

6. Only those members of the national organization who resided in the Middle west attended the conference in Chicago.   6.____

7. We told him to give the investigation assignment to whoever was available.   7.____

8. Please do not disappoint and embarass us by not appearing in court.   8.____

171

Questions 9-13

DIRECTIONS: Each of Questions 9 through 13 consists of three sentences lettered A, B, and C. In each of these questions, one of the sentences may contain an error in grammar, sentence structure, or punctuation, or all three sentences may be correct. If one of the sentence in a question contains an error in grammar, sentence structure, or punctuation, print in the space at the right the capital letter preceding the sentence which contains the error. If all three sentences are correct, print the letter D.

9. A. Mr. Smith appears to be less competent than I in performing these duties.
    B. The supervisor spoke to the employee, who had made the error, but did not reprimand him.
    C. When he found the book lying on the table, he immediately notified the owner.

    9.____

10. A. Being locked in the desk, we were certain that the papers would not be taken.
    B. It wasn't I who dictated the telegram; I believe it was Eleanor.
    C. You should interview whoever comes to the office today.

    10.____

11. A. The clerk was instructed to set the machine on the table before summoning the manager.
    B. He said that he was not familiar with those kind of activities.
    C. A box of pencils, in addition to erasers and blotters, was included in the shipment of supplies.

    11.____

12. A. The supervisor remarked, "Assigning an employee to the proper type of work is not always easy."
    B. The employer found that each of the applicants were qualified to perform the duties of the position.
    C. Any competent student is permitted to take this course if he obtains the consent of the instructor.

    12.____

13. A. The prize was awarded to the employee whom the judges believed to be most deserving.
    B. Since the instructor believes his book is the better of the two, he is recommending it for use in the school.
    C. It was obvious to the employees that the completion of the task by the scheduled date would require their working overtime.

    13.____

Questions 14-20.

DIRECTIONS: In answering Questions 14 through 20, choose the sentence which is BEST from the point of view of English usage suitable for a business report.

14. A. The client's receiving of public assistance checks at two different addresses were disclosed by the investigation.
    B. The investigation disclosed that the client was receiving public assistance checks at two different addresses.
    C. The client was found out by the investigation to be receiving public assistance checks at two different addresses.
    D. The client has been receiving public assistance checks at two different addresses, disclosed the investigation.

14.____

15. A. The investigation of complaints are usually handled by this unit, which deals with internal security problems in the department.
    B. This unit deals with internal security problems in the department usually investigating complaints.
    C. Investigating complaints is this unit's job, being that it handles internal security problems in the department.
    D. This unit deals with internal security problems in the department and usually investigates complaints.

15.____

16. A. The delay in completing this investigation was caused by difficulty in obtaining the required documents from the candidate.
    B. Because of difficulty in obtaining the required documents from the candidate is the reason that there was a delay in completing this investigation.
    C. Having had difficulty in obtaining the required documents from the candidate, there was a delay in completing this investigation.
    D. Difficulty in obtaining the required documents from the candidate had the affect of delaying the completion of this investigation.

16.____

17. A. This report, together with documents supporting our recommendation, are being submitted for your approval.
    B. Documents supporting our recommendation is being submitted with the report for your approval.
    C. This report, together with documents supporting our recommendation, is being submitted for your approval.
    D. The report and documents supporting our recommendation is being submitted for your approval.

17.____

18. A. The chairman himself, rather than his aides, has reviewed the report.
    B. The chairman himself, rather than his aides, have reviewed the report.
    C. The chairmen, not the aide, has reviewed the report.
    D. The aide, not the chairmen, have reviewed the report.

18.____

19. A. Various proposals were submitted but the decision is not been made.
     B. Various proposals has been submitted but the decision has not been made.
     C. Various proposals were submitted but the decision is not been made.
     D. Various proposals have been submitted but the decision has not been made.

20. A. Everyone were rewarded for his successful attempt.
     B. They were successful in their attempts and each of them was rewarded.
     C. Each of them are rewarded for their successful attempts.
     D. The reward for their successful attempts were made to each of them.

21. The following is a paragraph from a request for departmental recognition consisting of five numbered sentences submitted to a Captain for review. These sentences may or may not have errors in spelling, grammar, and punctuation:
     (1) The officers observed the subject Mills surreptitiously remove a wallet from the woman's handbag and entered his automobile. (2) As they approached Mills, he looked in their direction and drove away. (3) The officers pursued in their car. (4) Mills executed a series of complicated manuvers to evade the pursuing officers. (5) At the corner of Broome and Elizabeth Streets, Mills stopped the car, got out, raised his hands and surrendered to the officers.
     Which one of the following BEST classifies the above with regard to spelling, grammar, and punctuation?
     A. 1, 2, and 3 are correct, but 4 and 5 have errors.
     B. 2, 3, and 5 are correct, but 1 and 4 have errors.
     C. 3, 4, and 5 are correct, but 1 and 2 have errors.
     D. 1, 2, 3, and 5 are correct, but 4 has errors.

22. The one of the following sentences which is grammatically PREFERABLE to the others is:
     A. Our engineers will go over your blueprints so that you may have no problems in construction.
     B. For a long time he had been arguing that we, not he, are to blame for the confusion.
     C. I worked on his automobile for two hours and still cannot find out what is wrong with it.
     D. Accustomed to all kinds of hardships, fatigue seldom bothers veteran policemen.

23. The MOST accurate of the following sentences is:
     A. The commissioner, as well as his deputy and various bureau heads, were present.
     B. A new organization of employers and employees have been formed.
     C. One or the other of these men have been selected.
     D. The number of pages in the book is enough to discourage a reader.

24. The MOST accurate of the following sentences is:
    A. Between you and me, I think he is the better man.
    B. He was believed to be me.
    C. Is it us that you wish to see?
    D. The winners are him and her.

24.____

KEY (CORRECT ANSWERS)

1. C
2. A
3. C
4. A
5. B

6. C
7. D
8. C
9. B
10. A

11. B
12. B
13. D
14. B
15. D

16. A
17. C
18. A
19. D
20. B

21. B
22. A
23. D
24. A

CRIMINAL INVESTIGATION

TECHNIQUE OF INTERVIEWS AND INTERROGATION

TABLE OF CONTENTS

		Page
1.	General	1
2.	Purpose of Interview	1
3.	Preparation for Interview	1
4.	Time of Interview	2
5.	Place of Interview	2
6.	Introduction of the Investigator	2
7.	Control Over Interviews	2
8.	Rights of Person Interviewed	2
9.	Attitude and Demeanor of Investigator	2
10.	Types of Approaches	3
11.	Interview of Complainants	3
12.	Interview of Victims	3
13.	Interview of Witnesses	3
14.	Types of Witnesses	4
15.	Assistance to Witnesses in Descriptions	4
16.	Credibility of Witnesses	4
17.	Evaluation During Interview	5
18.	Interview Notes	5
19.	Purpose of Interrogation	5
20.	Preparation for Interrogation	6
21.	Classification of Suspects	6
22.	Length of Interrogation	6
23.	Persons at Interrogation	7
24.	Interrogation Checklist	7
25.	Introduction of Investigator	7
26.	Rights of Person Being Interrogated	7
27.	Attitude of Investigator	8
28.	Types of Approach	8
29.	Interrogation Notes	9
30.	Scientific Aids to Interrogation	9
31.	Lie Detecting Set	9
32.	Narco-Analysis	10

CRIMINAL INVESTIGATION

TECHNIQUE OF INTERVIEWS AND INTERROGATION

1. **GENERAL**
   The successful investigation of criminal offenses depends in a great measure upon the effective questioning of complainants, witnesses, informants, suspects, and other persons encountered during the course of an investigation. Questioning is divided into two broad classifications: *interviews*, which are conducted to learn facts from persons who may have knowledge of a wrongful act but who are not themselves implicated; and *interrogations*, which are conducted to learn facts and to obtain admissions or confessions of wrongful acts from persons who are implicated in a wrongful act. Persons who have been interviewed may later be interrogated. An interrogation is not necessarily confined to individuals suspected of criminal acts, but may include persons who may have been accessories, or who may have knowledge of the crime which, for various motives, they are reluctant to admit. It is usually advisable to take statements from persons being interviewed or interrogated. When an interview or interrogation develops information that will have definite value as evidence, that information or evidence must be recorded in a written, signed, and witnessed statement, or preserved through mechanical recording.

2. **PURPOSE OF INTERVIEW**
   An interview is an informal questioning to learn facts. The successful investigation of crime requires that the investigator be able to learn, through personal questioning, what the person interviewed has observed through his five senses: sight, hearing, taste, smell, and touch. Each individual interviewed is presumed to possess certain information that may lead to the solution of a crime. Effective interviewing requires that the interviewer make full use of all the knowledge of human nature he possesses, so that the individual interviewed will disclose all that he knows about the matter in question. If a person does not possess knowledge of the crime, the interview should establish that fact. Pertinent negative evidence is as much a part of a complete investigation as positive information.

3. **PREPARATION FOR INTERVIEW**
   Interviews other than those conducted at the scene of the crime should be planned carefully and thoroughly to prevent repetition of the interview. The investigator must review thoroughly all developments in the investigation prior to the interview. He must also consider the relationship of the person to be interviewed to the investigation; i.e., complainant, victim, witness, or informant. An effective interviewer combines his knowledge of human nature with all available information about the person to be interviewed, such as education, character, reputation, associates, habits, and past criminal record. This background information is used advantageously in the interview. The investigator should estimate the extent and kind of information that he may expect to elicit. He should prepare, by noting pertinent facts to be developed, to detect inconsistencies and discrepancies in the statements of the person being interviewed, to evaluate them, and to require their clarification. The investigator should prepare a plan for the interview

which takes into consideration the information available to him about the person to be interviewed: the time, place, and environment for the interview; as well as the legal proof to be developed in the crime.

4. **TIME OF INTERVIEW**
An interview should be conducted as soon as possible after the discovery of a crime. The investigator should take as much time as is required for a complete and thorough interview.

5. **PLACE OF INTERVIEW**
When possible, the place of the interview should be so selected as to assure a favorable environment. When possible, the interview should be conducted in a comfortable room and in an environment familiar to the person interviewed. The person to be interviewed should never be brought to the investigator.

6. **INTRODUCTION OF THE INVESTIGATR**
Usually the investigator and the person to be interviewed are strangers. The investigator should introduce himself, present his credentials (when appropriate), and begin by making a general statement regarding the purpose of the interview. The introduction should be made in such a manner as to establish a cordial relationship between the investigator and the person being interviewed.

7. **CONTROL OVER INTERVIEWS**
An investigator must maintain absolute control of the interview at all times. He must be careful not to elicit false information through improper questioning. He may permit digression or discussion of matters seemingly unrelated to the crime in order to place the person interviewed at ease but he must not permit the person being interviewed to become evasive. If the person interviewed should become so evasive as to obscure the purpose of the interview, effective results may be obtained by a more formal type of questioning, taking notes, or by the aggressiveness of the investigator.

8. **RIGHTS OF PERSON INTERVIEWED**
Although an investigator has no legal power to compel a person being interviewed to divulge information, he may, if he is clever and alert, induce him to disclose what he knows. When an interview develops into an interrogation, the investigator must warn the person being interviewed of his rights (Par. 26).

9. **ATTITUDE AND DEMEANOR OF INVESTIGATOR**
The attitude and demeanor of an investigator contributes immeasurably to the success or failure of an interview. The investigator should be friendly, yet businesslike. He should endeavor to lead the person being interviewed into talkativeness. He should then direct the conversation toward the investigation. The individual being interviewed should be permitted to give an uninterrupted account while the investigator makes mental notes of omissions, inconsistencies, or discrepancies that require clarification by later questioning. The investigator should strive to turn to advantage the subject's prejudices. He rarely reveals the precise objective of an interview, and usually obtains a more accurate account

from the person interviewed if he claims only to be attempting to establish facts. He should avoid a clash of personalities; acts of undue familiarity; the use of profanity or violent expressions such as "kill," "steal," "confess," "murder"; improbable stories; or distracting mannerisms such as pacing the floor or fumbling with objects.

10. **TYPES OF APPROACHES**

The *indirect* approach employed in interviewing consists of discussion carried on in a conversational tone that permits the person being interviewed to talk without having to answer direct questions. The *direct* approach consists of direct questioning as in interrogations (Par. 28a). The use of interrogation technique often succeeds when the person interviewed fears or dislikes police officers, fears retribution from a criminal, desires to protect a friend or relative, is impudent, or, for diverse reasons, is unwilling to cooperate with the investigator. Unreliable persons or liars should always be permitted to give their version of an incident. They may, through contradiction or denial, trip themselves into admissions through which the true facts may be obtained. When interviewing shy or nervous persons, the investigator may be obliged to obtain information piecemeal. He should interview in the normal environment of such persons and should be as casual and calm as possible. The talkative person should be allowed to speak freely and to use his own expressions, but should be confined to the subject by appropriate questions. When persons pretend to know nothing about an incident, the investigator should ask many questions, any one which, if answered, will refute their claim that they know nothing at all. Disinterested persons may divulge more information if their personal interest can be aroused by an indirect approach. Investigators should always attempt to put uneducated witnesses at ease and to help them express themselves as best they can, but should not put word into their mouths. Flattery is most often successful when alcoholics or braggarts are interviewed. Information gained from such individuals must be corroborated.

11. **INTERVIEW OF COMPLAINANTS**

In interviewing complainants, the investigator should be considerate, understanding, tactful, and impartial, regardless of the motive for the complaint, and should inform the complainant that appropriate action will be initiated promptly.

12. **INTERVIEW OF VICTIMS**

When interviewing victims, the investigator must consider their emotional state, particularly in crimes of violence. Frequently, victims have unsupported beliefs regarding the circumstances connected with the crime. Their observations may be partial and imperfect because of excitement and tension. It is imperative that the investigator obtain from the victim an accurate account of the circumstances that existed immediately before, during, and after the incident. The investigator should consider the reputation of the victim in determining the credibility of his complaint.

13. **INTERVIEW OF WITNESSES**

The investigator must frequently assist witnesses to recall and relate facts exactly as they observed them. He must know what affect a person's ability to observe and describe acts, articles, or circumstances related to a crime (CH. 3). He should lead witnesses toward accurate statements of fact by assisting them to recall in detail their experiences.

14. **TYPES OF WITNESSSES**

In general, children from 7 to 12 years of age are good observers, although their testimony may be inadmissible in court. Teenage children are also good observers but may exaggerate. Young adults are often poor witnesses; middle-aged and older persons are the best witnesses. Persons differ in their physical and mental characteristics as well as in their experience and training. These differences may cause them to notice only those aspects of a situation in which they may have had a particular experience. As a consequence, they differ in their observations, interpretations, and descriptions. If a witness cannot recall what he has observed, poor memory may be the cause. Preoccupation of a witness may often prevent him from recalling exactly what occurred. Lack of education may make it difficult for a witness to describe what he observed; such a person is sometimes reluctant to divulge information because of embarrassment over his diction. That which has been observed, because of exaggeration, misrepresentation, or inaccurate interpretation, may result in faulty information; i.e., a squeal of joy may be misinterpreted as a scream of terror. The emotions of witnesses before, during, and after an incident, and when interviewed, greatly affect their recall of events as they actually occurred. A frightened witness may recall events differently than a calm, unruffled person. Witnesses may exaggerate more each time their observations are repeated.

15. **ASSISTANCE TO WITNESSES IN DESCRIPTIONS**

The investigator should provide certain indexes to assist witnesses in describing size, height, weight, distance, and colors. The eye-level method of determining height may be used as standard. By asking a witness to tell how far another person's eyes were above or below his own, the investigator may obtain an estimate of height. Speed is difficult to estimate accurately; even opinions based on long experience may be subject to influence by noise, light, weather, and other conditions. Age is difficult for witnesses to judge because of differences among races, nationalities, and individuals; if selected individuals are used for comparison, they must be chosen carefully. In situations which are strange or which involve unusual circumstances, the witness may have no standards or associations on which to base his judgment and may be unable to utilize the standards presented for comparison. A detailed review or reconstruction of events will sometimes help the witness to recall events, but the investigator must be careful to avoid confusing the actual event with the reconstruction.

16. **CREDIBILITY OF WITNESSES**

Credibility of a witness is usually governed by his character and is evidenced by his reputation for veracity. Personal or financial reason or previous criminal activity may cause a witness to give false information to avoid being implicated. Hope of gain by informants or prisoners; political, racial, or religious factors; and hatred for the police or the suspect are some of the reasons why a witness may make a false statement. Age, sex, physical and mental abnormalities, loyalty, revenge, social and economic status, indulgence in alcohol, and the influence of other persons are some of the many factors which may affect the accuracy, willingness, or ability with which witnesses observe, interpret, and describe occurrences.

17. **EVALUATION DURING INTERVIEW**

    During an interview, the investigator must evaluate continuously the mannerisms and the emotional state of the person in terms of the information developed. The manner in which a person relates his story or answers questions may indicate that he is not telling the truth or is concealing information. Evasiveness, hesitation, or unwillingness to discuss situations may signify a lack of cooperation. The relation of body movements to the emotional state of persons must be carefully considered by the investigator. A dry mouth indicated by the wetting of the lips, fidgeting, or vague movements of the hands may indicate nervousness or deception. A "cold sweat" or pale face may indicate fear. A slight gasp, holding the breath, or an unsteady voice may indicate that the knowledge of the investigator has shocked the person being interviewed. The pumping of the heart may be observed by the pulse in the neck. A ruddy or flushed face may be an indication of anger or embarrassment, not necessarily guilt, and may also indicate that the matter under discussion is of vital importance, or that some information is being withheld. Although such symptoms are not necessarily valid indications of guilt or innocence and may be a manifestation of the physical condition or health of the individual, they are often related to the emotional state of the person.

18. **INTERVIEW NOTES**

    Complete notes are essential to effective investigation and reporting. Normally, most people have no objection to note-taking; however, the investigator should not take notes until he has had an opportunity to gage the person's reactions, since note-taking may create a reluctance to divulge information. If he does not take notes, the investigator should record, at the first opportunity after the interview, all pertinent information while it is fresh in his mind. Notes on interviews should contain the case number; hour, date, and place of interview; complete identification of the person interviewed; names of other persons present; and a resume of the interview.

19. **PURPOSE OF INTERROGATION**

    The interrogation should take place immediately if the suspect is surprised or apprehended in the act of committing a crime. In all other instances, interrogation should be conducted only after sufficient information has been secured and the background of the suspect has been thoroughly explored. The purpose of interrogation of a suspect is to obtain an admission or confession of his wrongful acts and a written, signed, and witnessed statement, and to establish the facts of a crime or to develop information which will enable the investigator to obtain direct, physical, or other evidence to prove or disprove the truth of an admission or confession. A confession is an acknowledgment of guilt, whereas an admission is a self-incriminatory statement falling short of an acknowledgment of guilt. The securing of confessions or acknowledgments of guilt does not complete the investigation of a crime. A statement made by one conspirator during the conspiracy and in pursuance of it is admissible in evidence against his co-conspirators as tending to prove the fact of the matter stated. In interrogation, the investigator seeks to learn the identity of accomplices and details of any other crime in which the suspect may have been involved.

20. **PREPARATION FOR INTERROGATION**
    a. Preparation for interrogation should be thorough. The investigator should base his plan for interrogation on background data, information, or direct evidence received from victims and witnesses, physical evidence, and reconstruction of the crime scene. The plan, which should be written, should take into consideration the various means for testing the truthfulness of the suspect and for gaining a psychological advantage over him through the use of known facts and proper use of time, place, and environment. Unless the investigator interrogates a suspect immediately following the commission of a crime, or desires to question him without previous notification, he should be interrogated at criminal investigation headquarters, where recordings may be made or stenographic notes may be taken.
    b. During interrogation, the subject should be seated in a plain chair placed where his movements and physical reactions may be observed easily. The interrogation room should be plainly but comfortably furnished, without items that may cause distraction. Recording devices, one-way mirrors, and similar equipment should appear as normal furnishings. Tables, desks, and other furnishings should be located where they will not impair the interrogator's observation of the suspect.

21. **CLASSIFICATION OF SUSPECTS**
    Background information and the facts established in an investigation enable the investigator to classify persons to be interrogated as follows:
    a. Known offenders, whose guilt is reasonably certain on the basis of the evidence available
    b. Persons whose guilt is doubtful or uncertain because of the evidence or lack of evidence.
    c. Material witnesses, accessories, and persons who have knowledge of the crime but may not themselves be guilty of a crime. Persons to be interrogated may be further classified as those readily influenced by sympathy or understanding; and those readily influenced by the use of an attitude of suspicion and obvious disbelief.

22. **LENGTH OF INTERROGATION**
    No time limit is placed on the duration of interrogation except that it shall not be so long and under such conditions as to amount to duress. Questioning for many hours without food, sleep, or under glaring lights has been held to constitute such duress as to invalidate a confession. The suspect may be questioned at length in an attempt to break down his resistance, or he may be questioned for short periods daily as a test of his consistency. The interrogator should always consider the physical condition of the person being interrogated as well as his emotional stability. Once the suspect has begun to reveal pertinent information, the interrogator should not be interrupted.

23. PERSONS AT INTERROGATION

An interrogation usually should be conducted in complete privacy. A person under interrogation is not inclined to reveal confidences to a public gathering. Witnesses to a confession may be called in to hear the reading of the statement and the declaration that it is the subject's statement, to witness the signing by the subject, and to affix their own signatures. Some investigative agencies advocate the presence of a witness at all times during an interrogation, particularly during the period of warning of rights and at such other periods when corroborative testimony might be needed or desirable. When a woman is questioned, the interrogator should provide witnesses, preferably women, in order to avoid charges of compromise which an unscrupulous woman may later interject a mitigating circumstance.

24. INTERROGATION CHECKLIST

Before beginning an interrogation, the investigator should check his preparation against the following questions:
  a. Has the crime scene been carefully and adequately searched for real evidence?
  b. Have all persons known to have knowledge of the crime been questioned?
  c. Has all possible evidence been obtained?
  d. Has the person to be interrogated been searched?
  e. Have all files been checked for pertinent information?
  f. Is background investigation complete?
  g. Is the interrogation room properly prepared for the interrogation?
  h. Is the interrogation plan complete?
  i. Have the elements of legal proof been checked?
  j. Are all details of the investigation firmly fixed in the investigator's mind?
  k. What information should be elicited from the individual to be interrogated?

25. INTRODUCTION OF INVESTIGATOR

Prior to any interrogation, the investigator may introduce and identify himself by presenting his credentials if the person to be interrogated questions the authority of the investigator. After the introduction, the person to be interrogated should be informed in general terms of the investigation being conducted. The investigator, however, should not disclose his knowledge of the case, nor should he prematurely disclose any fact of the case.

26. RIGHTS OF PERSON BEING INTERROGATED

The investigator should begin interrogation by explaining to the person to be questioned his rights under the Fifth Amendment to the Constitution of the United States. If he is a civilian, and under Article 31 of the Uniform Code of Military Justice, if he is a military person. The person to be questioned is informed that he need not answer any question which may tend to incriminate him but that, if he chooses to answer any question, such answer may be used in testimony against him. Throughout the questioning the investigator must refrain from threats, violence, or promise of reward. In response to a request by the person being questioned for legal counsel, the investigator should courteously but firmly refuse and state that the Uniform Code of Military Justice does not provide for counsel prior to charges being preferred against a soldier.

27. ATTITUDE OF INVESTIGATOR

Because of the importance of admissions or confessions, the investigator must become skilled in the art of interrogation. He must master a variety of questioning techniques, learn to judge the psychological strength of weakness of others, and learn to take advantage of his own particular abilities in questioning any suspect or reluctant witness. He must not presume guilt of the persons being interrogated without sufficient proof. He must act as naturally as possible under the circumstances. If a suspect begins admitting criminal acts, the investigator must not become overeager or condescending. The interrogator should, when it is necessary to stir the emotions of another to confess a wrongful act, permit his own emotions to be stirred.

28. TYPES OF APPROACH

He adapts his approach to the character and background of the person to be interrogated, the known facts of the crime, and the real evidence available. The investigator may use any of the following type approaches or any combination of them:

a. The *direct approach* is normally employed where guilt is reasonably certain. The investigator assumes an air of confidence concerning the guilt of the offender and points out the evidence indicative of guilt. He outwardly sympathizes with the offender and indicates that anyone else might have done the same thing under similar circumstances. He urges the offender to tell the truth, avoids threatening words or insinuation, and develops a detailed account of the crime from premeditation to commission. He may ask questions such as the following: "Tell me all you know about this. When did you get the idea of doing it? Why did you do it? How did you do that? Where did you get the money?" In dealing with habitual criminals whose guilt is reasonably certain and who apparently have no feeling of wrongdoing, the investigator must convince them that their guilt can be or is established by the testimony of witnesses or available evidence. Investigators must never make promises of leniency or clemency as these promises might vitiate confessions obtained as a result of the interrogation.

b. The *indirect approach* is normally employed in interrogating a person who has knowledge of the crime. The investigator must proceed cautiously. He requests the individual being interrogated to tell all he knows about the incident. He then requires an explanation of discrepancies or distortions and endeavors to lead the individual being interrogated into admissions of truth. When facts indicative of guilt are developed, the investigator casually asks question to determine through the offender's reactions whether he will acknowledge or deny guilt. When guilt appears probable, the investigator reverts to direct questioning to obtain an admission or confession.

c. The *emotional approach* is designed to arouse any play upon the emotions of a person. Body actions may indicate the presence of nervous tension. The investigator points out these signs of nervous tension to the person under interrogation. The investigator may discuss the moral seriousness of the offense, emphasize the penalty, and appeal to the suspect's pride or ego, fear, like or dislike, or his hate and desire for revenge. This approach may lead to emotional breakdown and a confession.

d. *Subterfuge* is employed to induce guilty persons to confess when all other approaches have failed. Considerable care should be exercised in the employment of subterfuge. If the person to be interrogated recognizes the approach as subterfuge, further efforts to obtain an admission or confession may be futile. Examples of subterfuge are:

(1) *Hypothetical Story.* A fictitious crime, varying only in minute details from the offense of which the subject is suspected, is related to him. The investigator later visits the subject and asks him to write out details of the hypothetical story as related. If the subject is guilty, he often includes details of the crime under investigation, but not mentioned by the investigator in his fictitious story. When confronted with these inconsistencies, the suspect may make a confession.

(2) *Signed False Statement.* When evidence indicates, but is not conclusive, that a certain person may be guilty of a crime, he may be requested to make a sworn written statement. After he has made a false written statement, the discrepancies contained therein are pointed out to him in an attempt to gain a true confession.

(3) *"Cold Shoulder."* This term designates a technique of subterfuge keynoted by indifference. The person suspected is invited to come to the investigator's office. If he accepts the invitation, he is taken either to the office or the crime scene. The investigator, or those accompanying the person subject to this type of interrogation, say nothing to him or to each other, and await his reactions. This technique may cause the suspect to surmise that the investigator has evidence adequate to prove his guilt.

(4) *Playing One Suspect Against Another.* When two or more persons are suspected of having been involved in a crime, the person believed to have the weakest character is interrogated first. The others are interrogated separately and informed that their partner has accused them of the crime. A confession, shown to the others involved, may influence them to attempt to protect themselves by confessing.

(5) *Contrasting Personalities.* This technique employs two investigators, one determined and the other sympathetic and understanding. The interrogation is so arranged that the person under interrogation will play into the hands of one or the other.

29. INTERROGATION NOTES

The taking of notes during an interrogation may be essential in order to record all pertinent information; however, the effect of note-taking on the success of the interrogation must be considered. If notes are not taken during the interrogation, the investigator should record all pertinent data immediately after the interrogation.

30. SCIENTIFIC AIDS TO INTEROGATION

Scientific aids are available to the investigator to assist in the investigation of criminal offenses. These aids are normally employed to develop information from persons who are suspected of committing a crime. They may also be used to check the validity and completeness of information given by complainants, witnesses, and victims.

31. LIE DETECTING SET

Lie detecting set examinations can be conducted only by operators trained in the use of the instrument. The lie detecting set is an instrument which records the body changes that accompany emotions and is used to develop information, to determine if a person has knowledge of an offense, and to obtain an admission or confession of guilt. The provisions of Article 31, Uniform Code of Military Justice, and the Fifth Amendment to the Constitution of the United States apply to persons who are requested to submit to an examination by a lie detecting set. Investigators should obtain written consent from all persons subjected to lie detecting set examinations, acknowledging that they have been informed of their rights and that they agree to submit voluntarily to such an examination. A copy of this statement should be included in the case file folder. In general, graphs obtained during a lie detecting set examination are not admissible as evidence in court. However, the operator is usually permitted to testify relative to the questions asked, and the answers given. Oral or written admissions or confessions obtained as a consequence of the examination may be admitted into evidence, if they meet legal requirements.

32. NARCO-ANALYSIS

Narco-analysis is the term employed to define the questioning of a person under the influence of drugs (truth serums). Scopolamine, sodium amytal, and sodium pentothal are the drugs most commonly used. When properly administered, these drugs tend to overcome inhibitions. The use of narco-analysis as an investigative technique has not found general acceptance. Admissions or confessions obtained through the use of truth serums are not admissible as evidence in court. The information obtained may be used only to develop the investigation. The subject must be warned of his rights, and a written statement obtained wherein the subject acknowledges the warning and voluntarily agrees to the narco-analysis. *No person may be compelled to submit to such an examination. It must be conducted only when a qualified medical officer if available to administer the drugs and to witness the examination.*